Published by Bassline Publishing
www.basslinepublishing.com

Copyright © Bassline Publishing 2024
International Copyright Secured. All rights reserved.
No part of this book may be copied or reproduced by any
means without written permission from the publisher.

ISBN: 978-1-7394909-7-3

BASS GYM

INTRODUCTION

Welcome to the eleventh book in the Bass Gym 101 series, a collection of books for bassists who want to push their playing to the next level. We've reached the magic number of 1111 exercises, covering all of the important aspects of bass playing: warm-ups using the finger-per-fret system, arpeggios, pentatonics, all types of scales, odd time signatures, slap bass, plectrum technique and chord playing. This book is a continuation of the book for absolute beginners.

In writing this book, my intention was to write fun, practical and, above all, *inspiring* exercises that will guide the student through the various positions on the fretboard. The bass guitar's fretboard is divided into four zones (or positions, if you prefer): from the open strings to the third fret (1st position), from the third to the sixth fret (2nd position), through the sixth to the ninth fret (3rd position) and finally from the ninth to the twelfth fret (4th position). In the second half of the book you will learn how to combine positions, and by the time you have completed all 101 exercises you should have a very detailed and effective knowledge of the fretboard from the open strings to the twelfth fret - this is the area in which the vast majority of the basslines you know so well from popular songs or musical styles take place.

Inside you will find 101 exercises that will take you through all the positions on the bass in a structured, logical sequence. These exercises will also get you playing in different musical styles, using the most common melodic and rhythmic patterns of popular basslines.

Each exercise is written in both standard notation and TAB, and audio files can be downloaded from the Bassline Publishing website. As the book is primarily aimed at beginner and intermediate players, you won't find any of the more demanding techniques such as hammer ons, pull offs, trills etc. However, each exercise has been written for a specific playing situation and is immediately applicable to music practice. I've paid close attention to melody, clear phrasing and of course playability. Each of these exercises will challenge your attention and memory as you repeat them.

You'll find basslines in many styles of music in this book: walking bass, hip hop, pop, rock, punk, ska, metal, progressive styles, various Afro-Cuban grooves, funk, indie, reggae, country and bluegrass, EDM styles, blues, soul and folk.

I wish you a lot of fun, patience and of course inspiration while learning the positions on the bass.

Marek Bero
August 2024
London, United Kingdom

MAREK BERO BIOGRAPHY

Bass guitar is my life. I've been playing since I was fifteen, I've been in countless bands and recording studios, and I've played thousands of gigs in clubs and festivals all over Europe (Sonisphere, Ozzfest, Simple Things, Dimensions, etc.). I've also been an artist for Yamaha basses, Ampeg and Markbass Ultimate & Advanced series strings for years.

Photo credit: Josh Trigg

Since 2011 I have been living in London, UK, where I continue my musical career as an MD, session player and tutor. Since 2019 I have been working with producers Andy Wright and Gavin Goldberg (Jeff Beck, Simple Minds, Massive Attack), who I met while working on the Punt Guns project, where I also made my first appearance as a composer, singer and lyricist.

In 2023 I recorded three tracks for Simply Red's album *Time*, and continued to play solo with my Low Heaven project. I also taught private lessons, and toured and recorded with various artists in the UK and Europe.

I am the author of other educational books, such as *Bass Guitar in Rock and Metal* (2011), *Bass Gym - 101 Warm-ups for Finger Independence* (2013), *Bass Gym - 101 Arpeggios for Melodic Bass Lines* (2016), *Bass Gym – 101 Pentatonics for Killer Grooves* (2018), *Bass Gym – 101 Scales for Mastering Fingerboard* (2018), *Bass Gym – 101 Jazz Scales for Rockers* (2019), *Bass Gym - 101 Basslines for Beginners* (2020), *Bass Gym - 101 Odd Time Grooves* (2020), *Bass Gym - 101 Essential Slap Grooves* (2021), *Bass Gym - 101 Essential Plectrum Grooves* (2022) and *Bass Gym - 101 Chords & Harmonic Accompaniments* (2023).

Personal website:
http://marekbero.co.uk

To contact me for private lessons, Skype lessons, consultations or to arrange a workshop, please email:
marekbero@gmail.com

BASS GYM

FRETBOARD ORIENTATION

You could be the most technically talented bassist in the world, but if you don't know your fretboard like the back of your hand, you will likely find it very difficult to move forward with your musical development.

Fretboard orientation is an essential skill, and I can't stress enough how important it is. You can skip reading music, but don't skip knowing the notes on the fretboard.

At first it might seem daunting to learn all of the notes in all of the positions. There are so many! However, there's no need to rush and you can break everything down into small parts and sections which will be much more intuitive for familiarising yourself with the fretboard. It's also worth remembering that the fretboard contains a lot of repetition.

For this reason, I have divided the fretboard in this book into four main sections:

- 1st position: the open strings up to the third fret.
- 2nd position: notes from the third to the sixth fret.
- 3rd position: notes from the sixth to the ninth fret.
- 4th position: notes from the ninth to the twelfth fret.

The book begins with exercises in 1st position and gradually works up to exercises in the 4th position. In the second half of the book we will then combine the movement between positions so that by the end we will have a smooth orientation and movement from the open strings to the twelfth fret.

But what about the tones and orientation on the fretboard from the twelfth fret onwards?

I've got good news for you: from the twelfth fret onwards, you already know all the notes because they're the same as they were in the lower part of the fretboard, just an octave higher.

This structure fretboard works perfectly with the finger-per-fret system. This is a very effective system both in terms of orientation and in terms of economical fretting hand movements and fingerings.

When playing in the lower part of the fretboard (below the fifth fret), it is sometimes more comfortable to use condensed fingering. This means covering a three-fret span with all four fingers. When using this system, intervals of fifths and octaves (which are very common in bass lines) can be fretted using the first and fourth fingers. This system works well for those with small hands, and avoids the excessive bending of the wrist that occurs when using the finger-per-fret system in lower positions. It is very useful to be able to move between the two fingering systems, as required.

BASS GYM

FRETBOARD POSITIONS - A GRAPHIC OVERVIEW

1st Position
2nd Position
3rd Position
4th Position

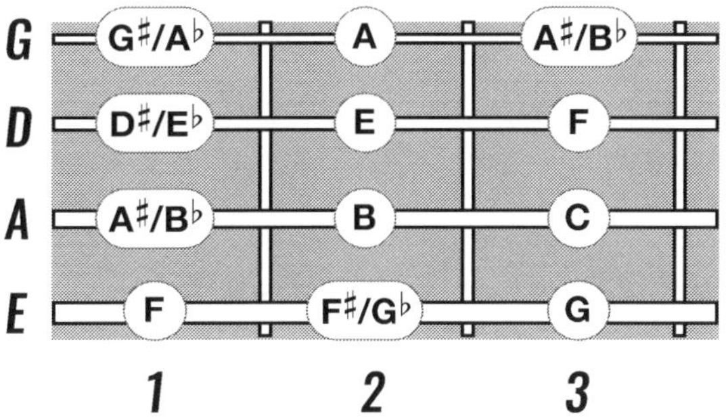

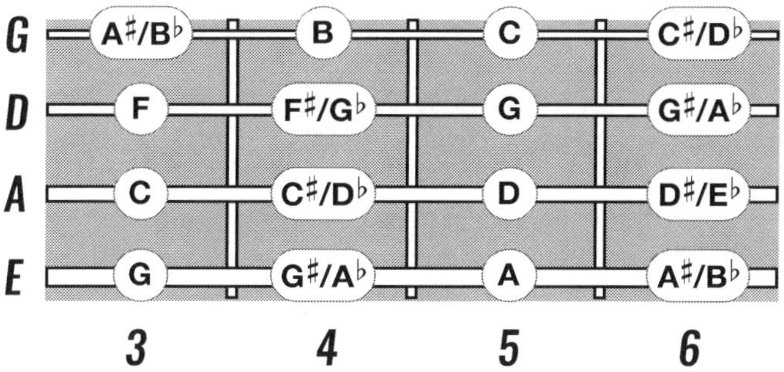

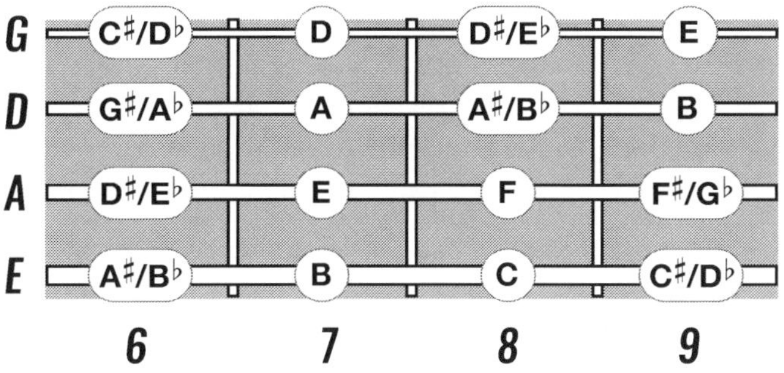

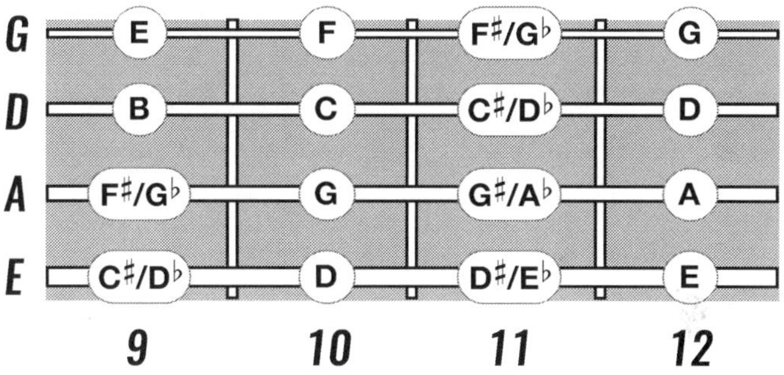

Remember that, as shown below, the notes above the twelfth fret are the same as they were in the lower part of the fingerboard:

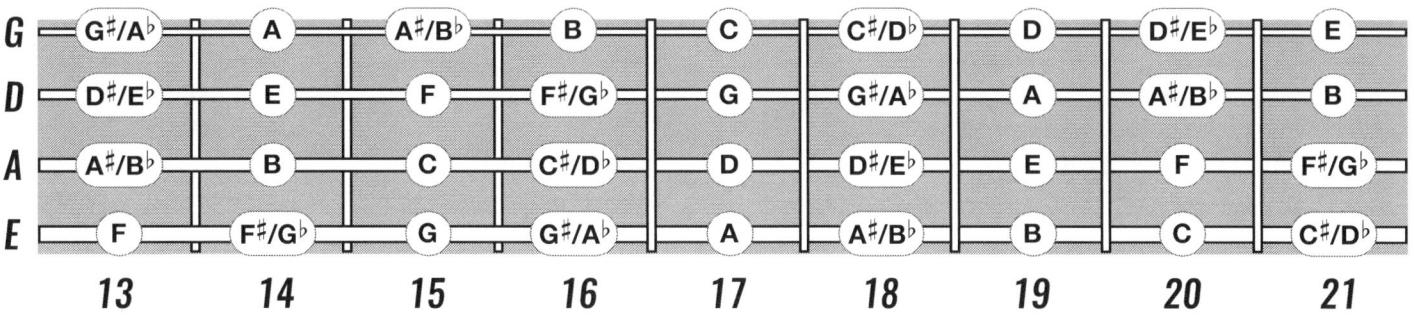

101 POSITION EXERCISES (BEGINNER & INTERMEDIATE LEVEL)

TIPS & TRICKS
TO IMPROVE FRETBOARD KNOWLEDGE

The Rule of Three
Every note can be found in many locations on the fretboard. Consider the fretboard in three sections: the open strings up to the fifth fret, the fifth fret to the twelfth (the middle register), and the twelfth fret and above (the upper register). If you play a G note at the third fret on the E-string, you can also play an octave above it (by pressing the fifth fret on the D-string with your little finger). This will cover the lowest position on the fretboard. Then find the G note in the middle register of the fretboard. Do you know where it is? The tenth fret of the A string. Again, add an octave (press the twelfth fret on the G string with your little finger). Finally, find the G in the upper register. It is located at the fifteenth fret on the E string and its octave at the seventeenth fret on the D string. Try to find everything you play in this way. If you play the bassline in a certain position in the band, are you able to play it in two other positions? Learning to do so will improve your ability to navigate the fretboard.

The Four Most Important Notes
Do you know where the notes for the open strings E, A, D and G are? Try to find them by following the procedure in the previous tip. These four notes are very, very important and I recommend that you become very familiar with their placement on the fingerboard. These so-called open strings harmonies are not only very popular for writing rock and metal riffs , but they are also common in many pop songs.

Consistent Fingerings
When you're learning a new bassline, exercise or groove, you should find a way to play the material as consistently as possible. Find the position and fingering that feels most comfortable and natural to you. Then, when you practise, don't make variations and play everything with the same fingers and using the same position on the fingerboard. This way you're building your muscle memory. Quick tip, in order to create an efficient fingering, try not shift with each finger more than twice in the position, otherwise your fingering will stutter. Once you have built up solid and effortless fingering you'll be able to play the material without having to constantly monitor your hand movements and you'll be well on your way to better performance, to play faster and smoother than if you were constantly changing the fingerings of your left hand.

WHAT TO DO WHEN IT SIMPLY DOESN'T WORK

Sometimes it just isn't your day: perhaps a particular exercise makes no sense, or doesn't fall easily under the fingers. You feel like you're struggling, and getting nowhere. It happens to everyone, even the most experienced players in the business. If this is the case, I recommend taking a break in order to clear your head. A bit of time away from the instrument (maybe go for a walk) will work wonders, and you'll usually come back to it with a fresh perspective.

If the setbacks are longer term and you don't see the desired improvement after a few months with this book, then you need to identify the problem. Do you need someone to guide you? Sometimes a few sessions with a professional tutor can work wonders. Suddenly you realise that all you had was bad technique, inefficient fingerings or a badly set up instrument. There can be any number of causes, but problems that could take you months to understand can sometimes be solved in just a few lessons.

Another cause of stagnation in your development can be too much focus on the technical elements of your playing. It might sound paradoxical, but if you focus solely on technique, you may miss the larger context of playing. Engage your ears, your heart, your vocal chords and your physical experience of the music. Try humming the exercises, whistling or clapping along with the rhythmic patterns. Remember that the **easiest way to become a better bassist is to become a better musician**. Relax, find your passion and joy for music and then put it all into your bass playing. You may find that everything suddenly goes a little better, you learn faster and the tone of your instrument suddenly has a surprisingly singing quality.

Learn to enjoy your practice time, and the process of learning a new skill. Most importantly, don't turn playing the bass into just another job.

BASS GYM

STRUCTURE AND METHODOLOGY

As in each volume of the Bass Gym 101 series, there are 101 exercises in this book.

Exercise methodology:

- Exercises 1-10: Exercises on open strings up to the third fret (1st position)
- Exercises 11-20: Exercises on the third to sixth fret (2nd position)
- Exercises 21-30: Exercises on the sixth to ninth fret (3rd position)
- Exercises 31-40: Exercises on the ninth to twelfth fret (4th position)
- Exercises 41-50: Combination of 1st and 2nd positions
- Exercises 51-60: Combination of 2nd and 3rd positions
- Exercises 61-70: Combination of 3rd and 4th positions
- Exercises 71-75: Skipping between 1st and 3rd positions
- Exercises 76-80: Skipping between 2nd and 4th positions
- Exercises 81-85: Skipping between 1st and 4th positions
- Exercises 86-101: Free movement between all positions

All exercises are available as MP3 downloads at this link: www.basslinepublishing.com/free-stuff

BASS GYM

1) Walking Bassline in F major

2) Hip-Hop Groove

101 POSITION EXERCISES (BEGINNER & INTERMEDIATE LEVEL)

BASS GYM

3) Pop Rock Bassline

4) 12-Bar Blues

10   101 POSITION EXERCISES (BEGINNER & INTERMEDIATE LEVEL)

BASS GYM

5) Rock Bassline

101 POSITION EXERCISES (BEGINNER & INTERMEDIATE LEVEL)

BASS GYM

6) Riff in the style of Chris Wolstenholme (Muse)

7) Funky Groove

12 101 POSITION EXERCISES (BEGINNER & INTERMEDIATE LEVEL)

BASS GYM

BASS GYM

12) Soul Bassline

101 POSITION EXERCISES (BEGINNER & INTERMEDIATE LEVEL)

BASS GYM

13) Funky Blues

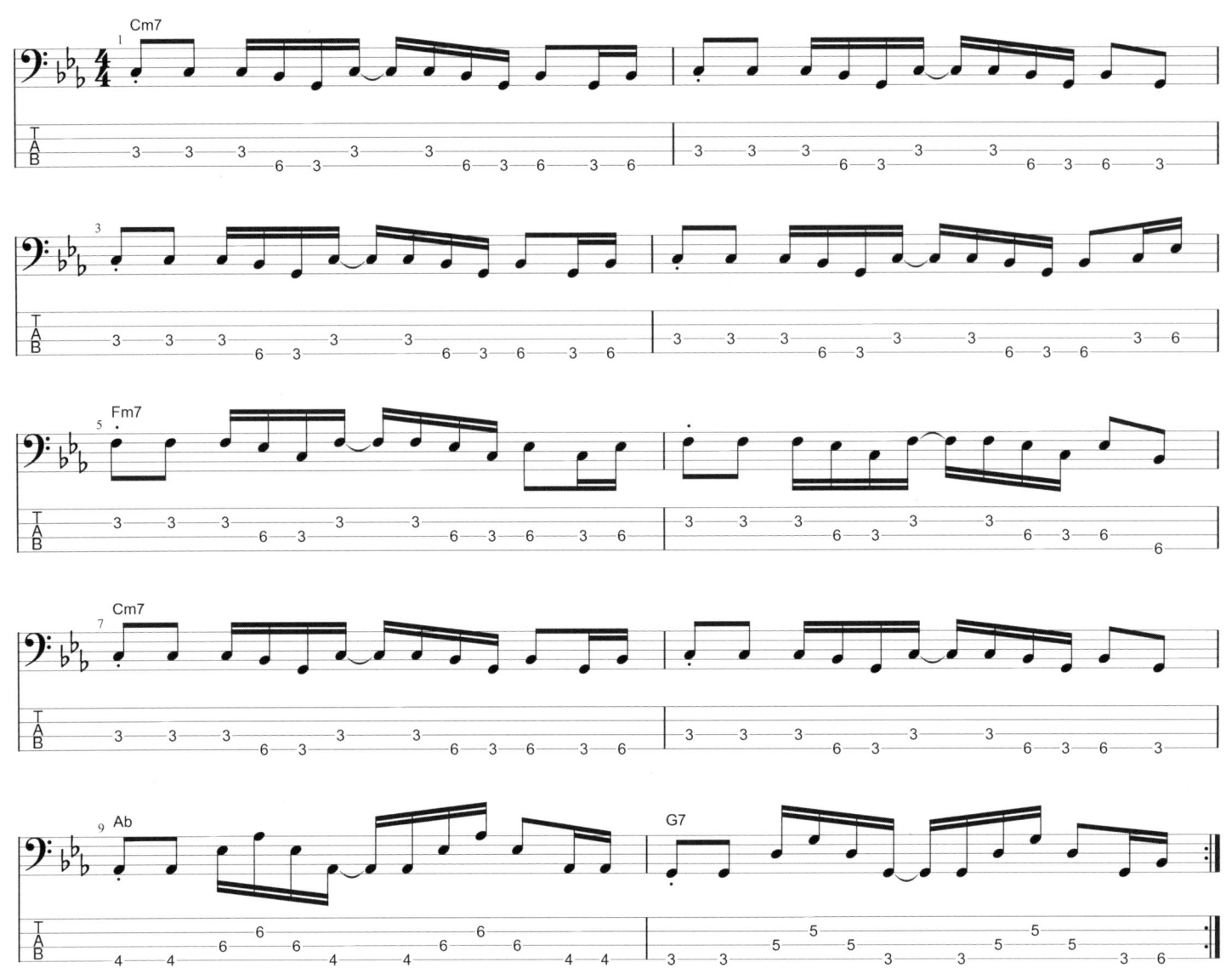

BASS GYM

14) Hard Rock Riffs

101 POSITION EXERCISES (BEGINNER & INTERMEDIATE LEVEL)

BASS GYM

15) Phrygian Heavy Metal Bassline

18 101 POSITION EXERCISES (BEGINNER & INTERMEDIATE LEVEL)

BASS GYM

16) Reggae Shuffle

101 POSITION EXERCISES (BEGINNER & INTERMEDIATE LEVEL)

BASS GYM

17) Salsa Variations

18) Salsa Variations

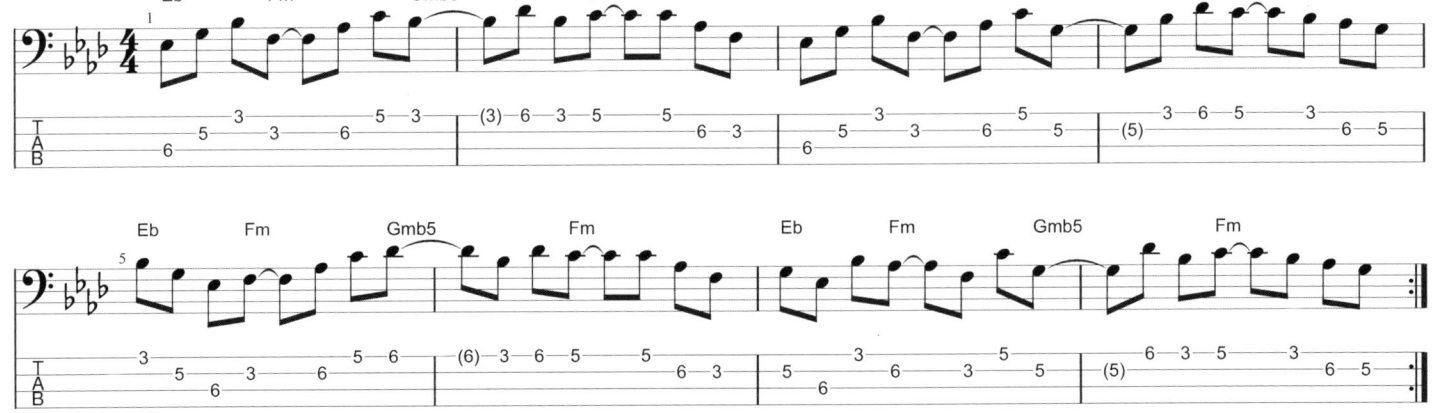

20 101 POSITION EXERCISES (BEGINNER & INTERMEDIATE LEVEL)

BASS GYM

19) Classical Etude (to practice the combination of the 3rd and 4th fingers in G minor)

20) Syncopated Groove

101 POSITION EXERCISES (BEGINNER & INTERMEDIATE LEVEL)

BASS GYM

21) Disco Funk Groove

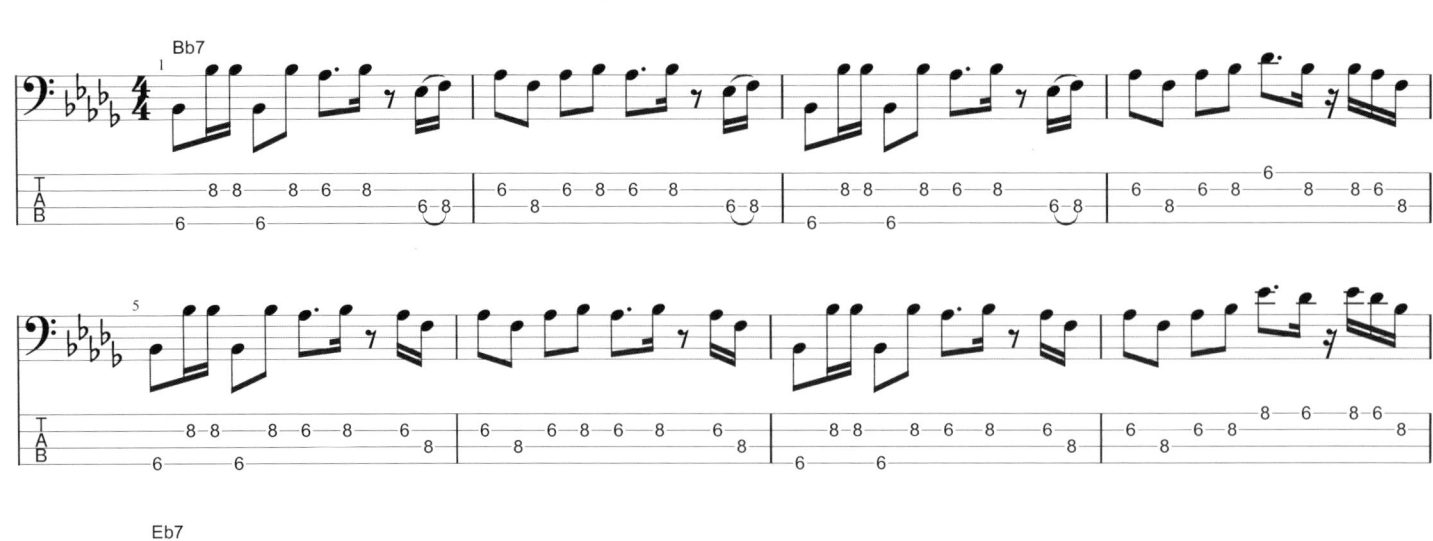

22 101 POSITION EXERCISES (BEGINNER & INTERMEDIATE LEVEL)

BASS GYM

22) Melodic Etude

101 POSITION EXERCISES (BEGINNER & INTERMEDIATE LEVEL)

BASS GYM

23) Funky Syncopated Groove

24 101 POSITION EXERCISES (BEGINNER & INTERMEDIATE LEVEL)

BASS GYM

24) Reggae Bassline

25) Sixteenth Note Syncopation

101 POSITION EXERCISES (BEGINNER & INTERMEDIATE LEVEL)

BASS GYM

26) Aeolian Ska Bassline

27) Bassline in the style of 'The Time of My Life' from the film Dirty Dancing

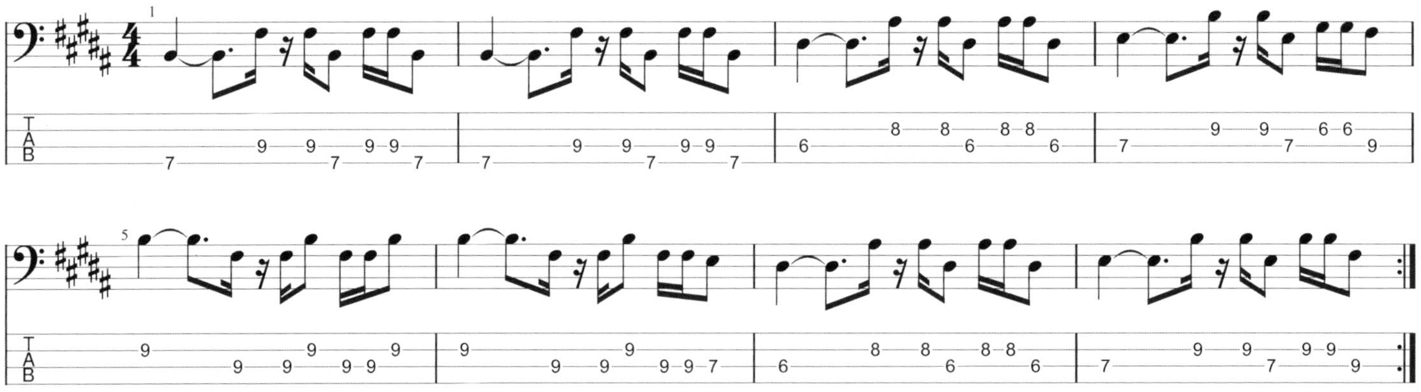

BASS GYM

28) Bass Riff with Minor Pentatonic Variations

101 POSITION EXERCISES (BEGINNER & INTERMEDIATE LEVEL)

BASS GYM

29) Rhythmic Funk Groove with Minor Pentatonic Variations

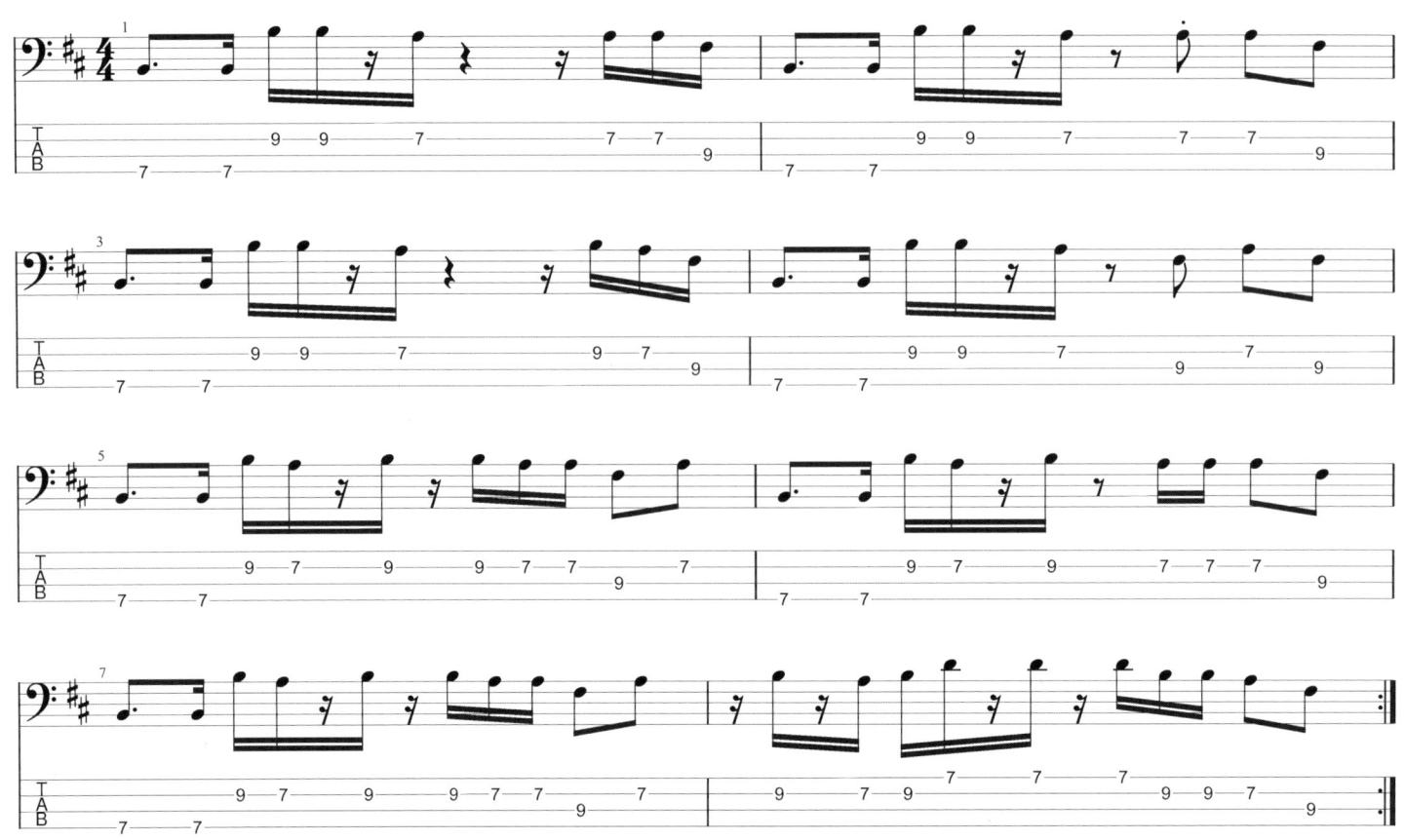

28   101 POSITION EXERCISES (BEGINNER & INTERMEDIATE LEVEL)

BASS GYM

30) 70s Soul Bassline

31) Salsa Bassline

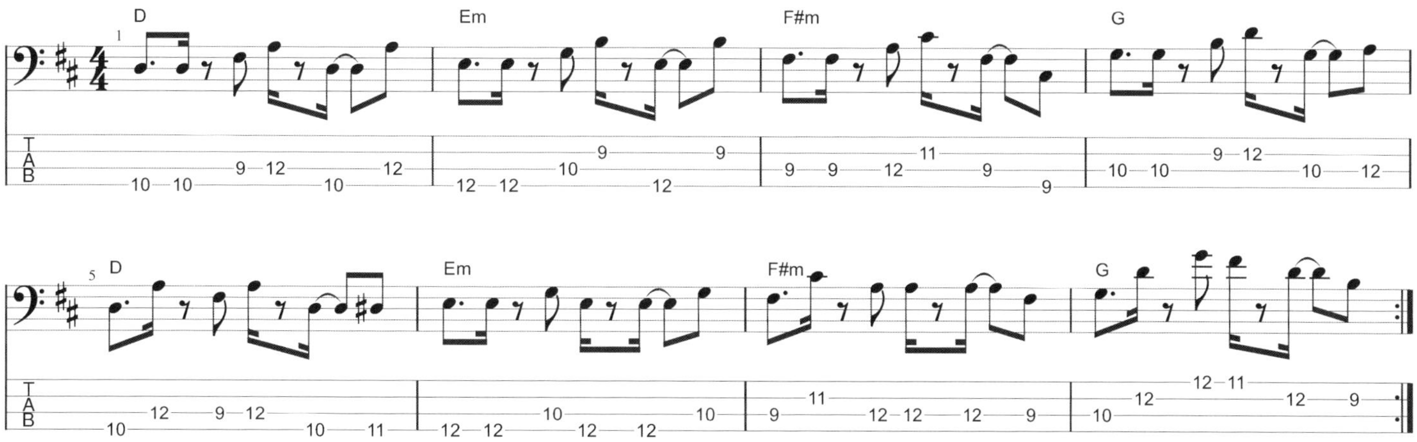

101 POSITION EXERCISES (BEGINNER & INTERMEDIATE LEVEL)

BASS GYM

32) Hip Hop Riff with Variations

33) Songo Bassline

BASS GYM

34) Classical Etude

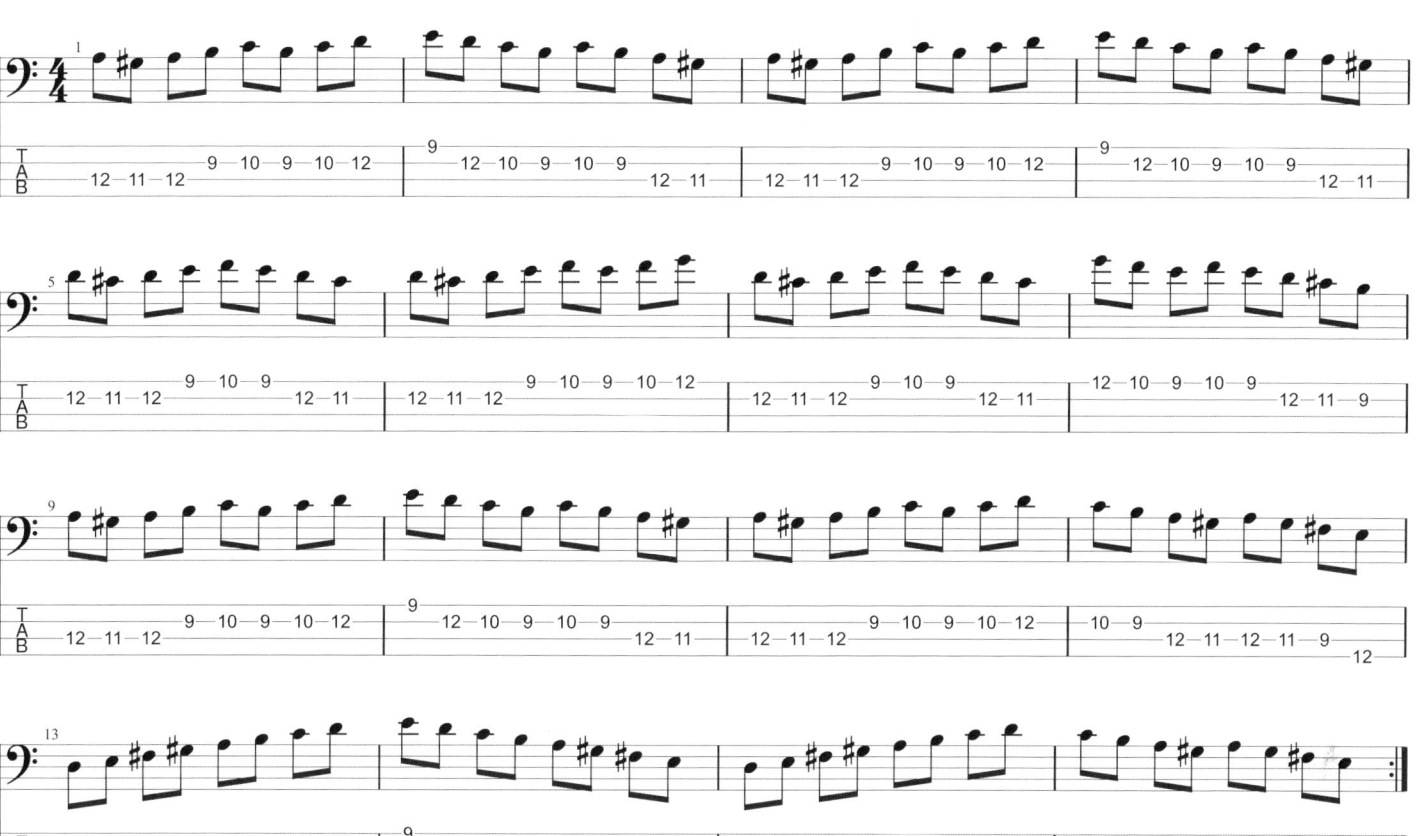

101 POSITION EXERCISES (BEGINNER & INTERMEDIATE LEVEL)

BASS GYM

35) Sixteenth Note Subdivision Practice

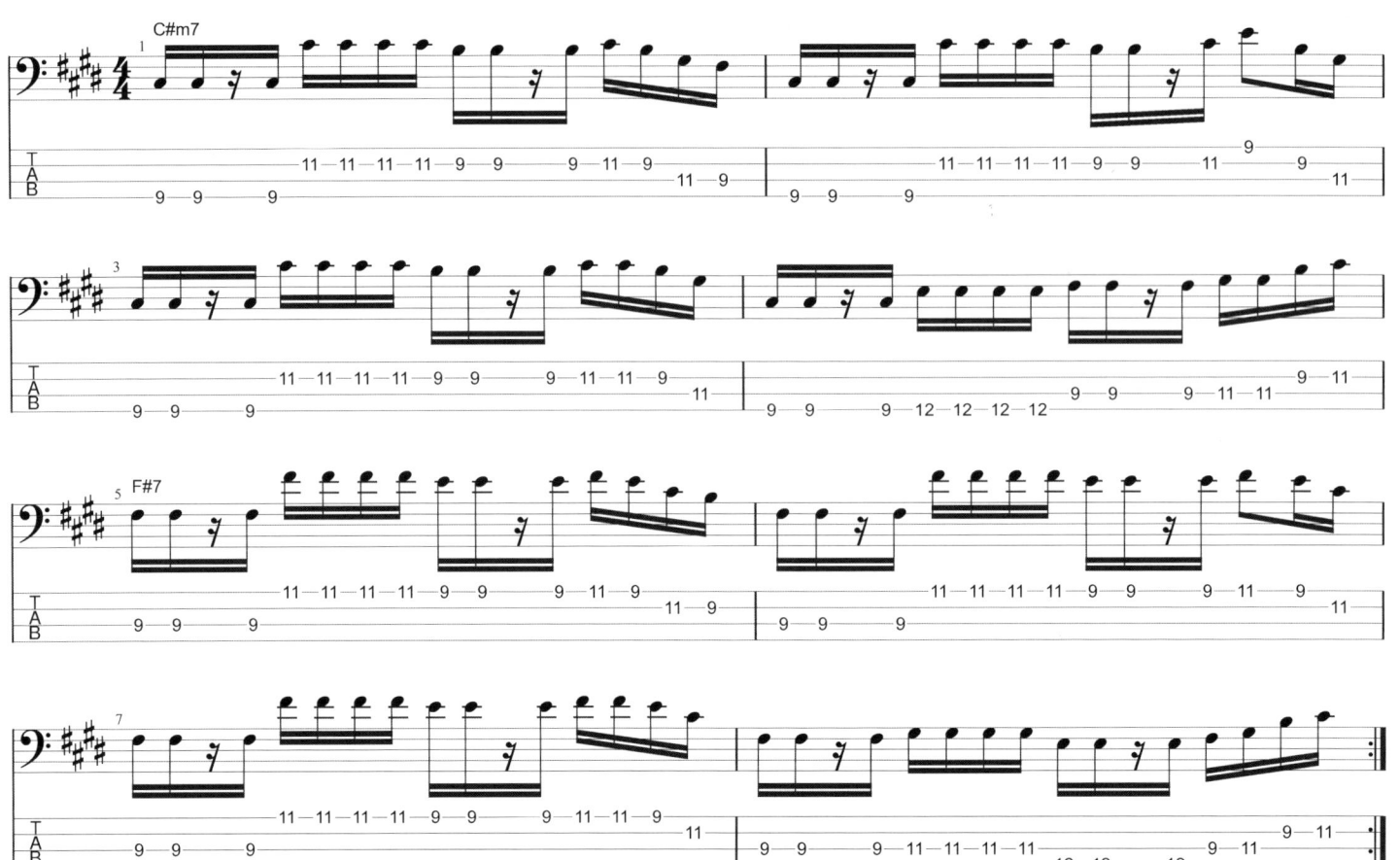

BASS GYM

36) Funk Bass Groove

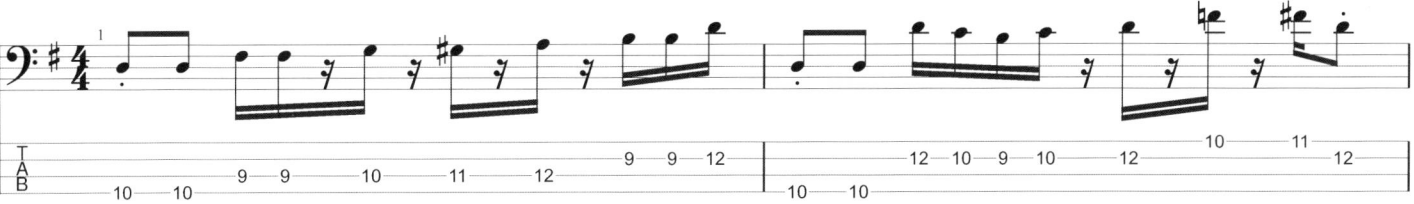
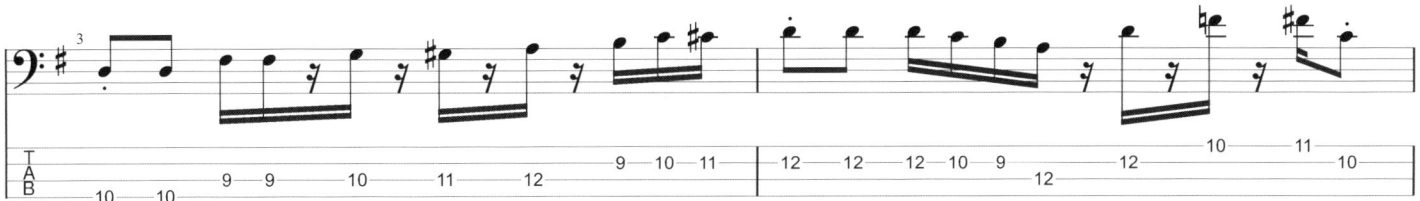
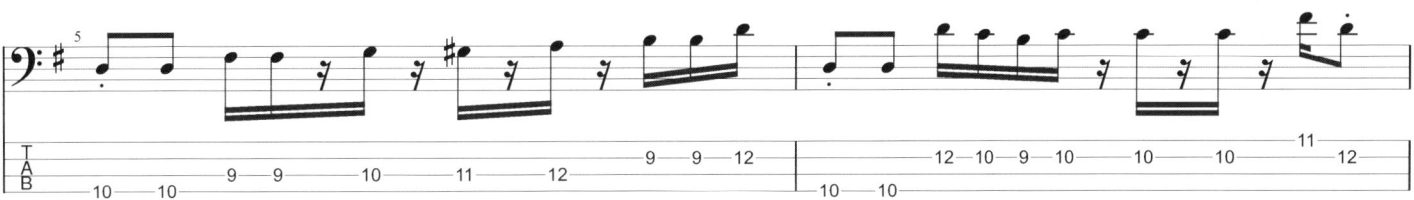
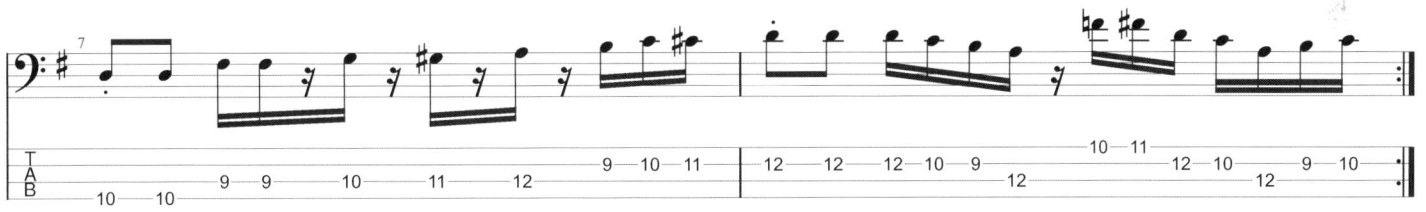

BASS GYM

37) Pop Punk Bassline with Rhythmic Variations

38) 12-Bar Blues

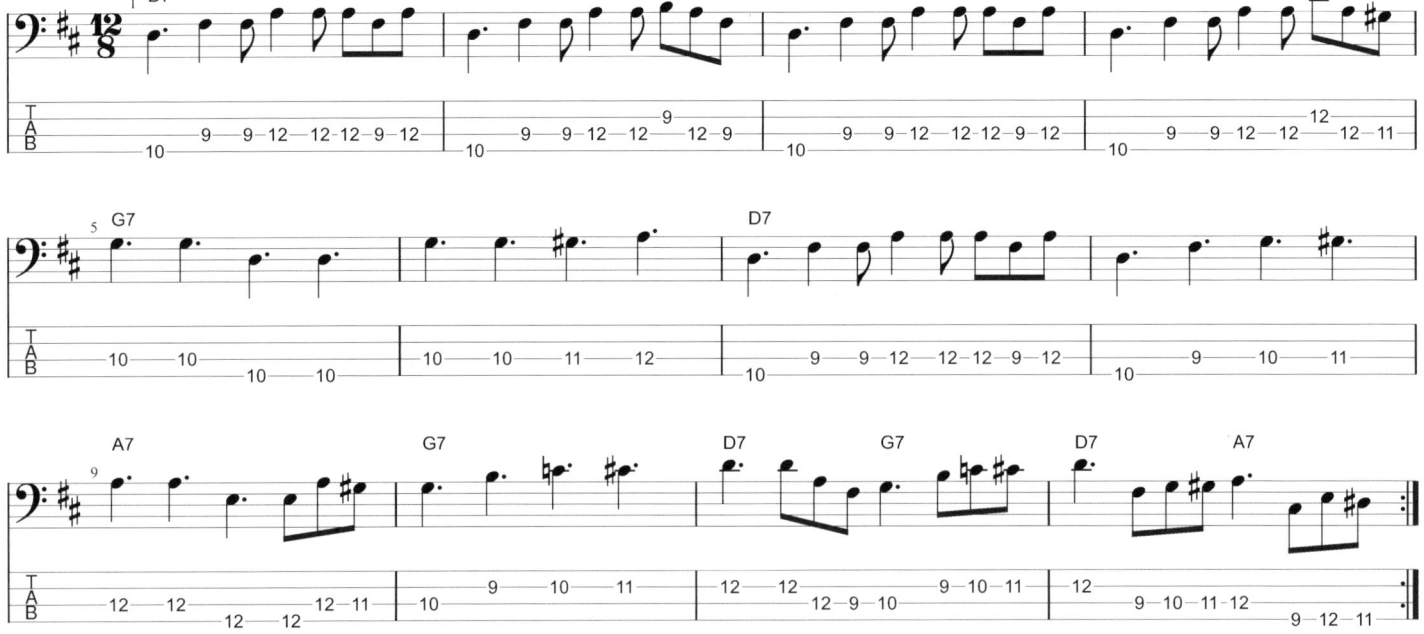

34 101 POSITION EXERCISES (BEGINNER & INTERMEDIATE LEVEL)

BASS GYM

39) Arpeggio Practice

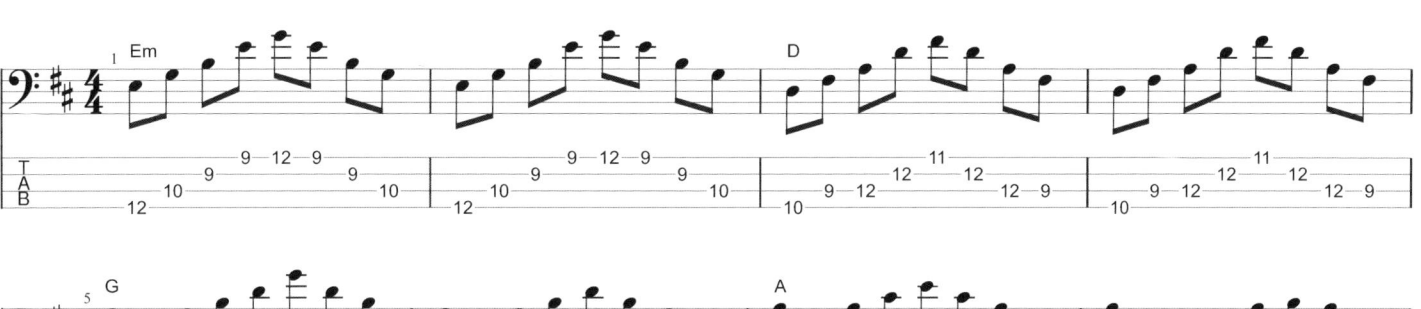
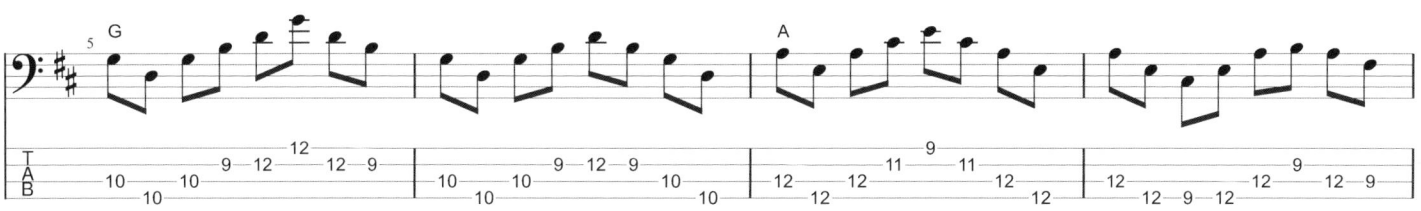
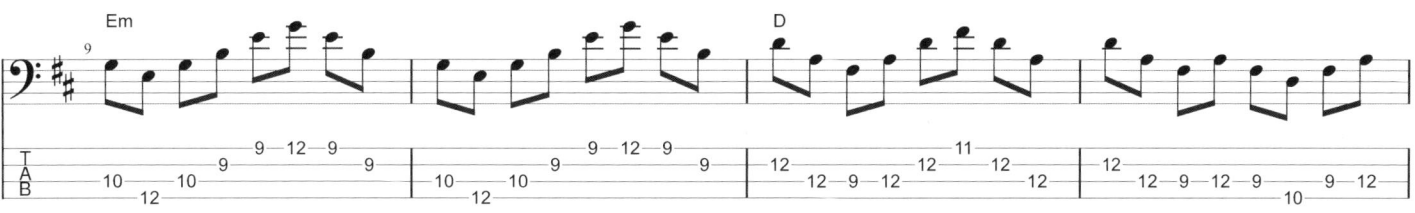
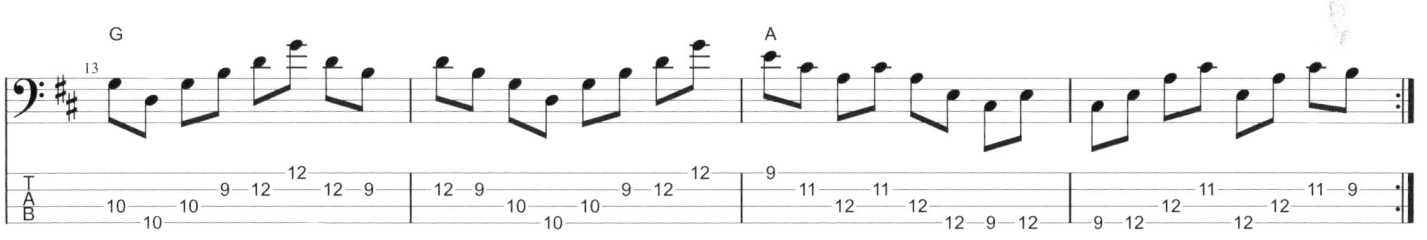

BASS GYM

40) R'n'B Dorian Riff

BASS GYM

41) Groove Metal Riff (Combination of 1st and 2nd Positions)

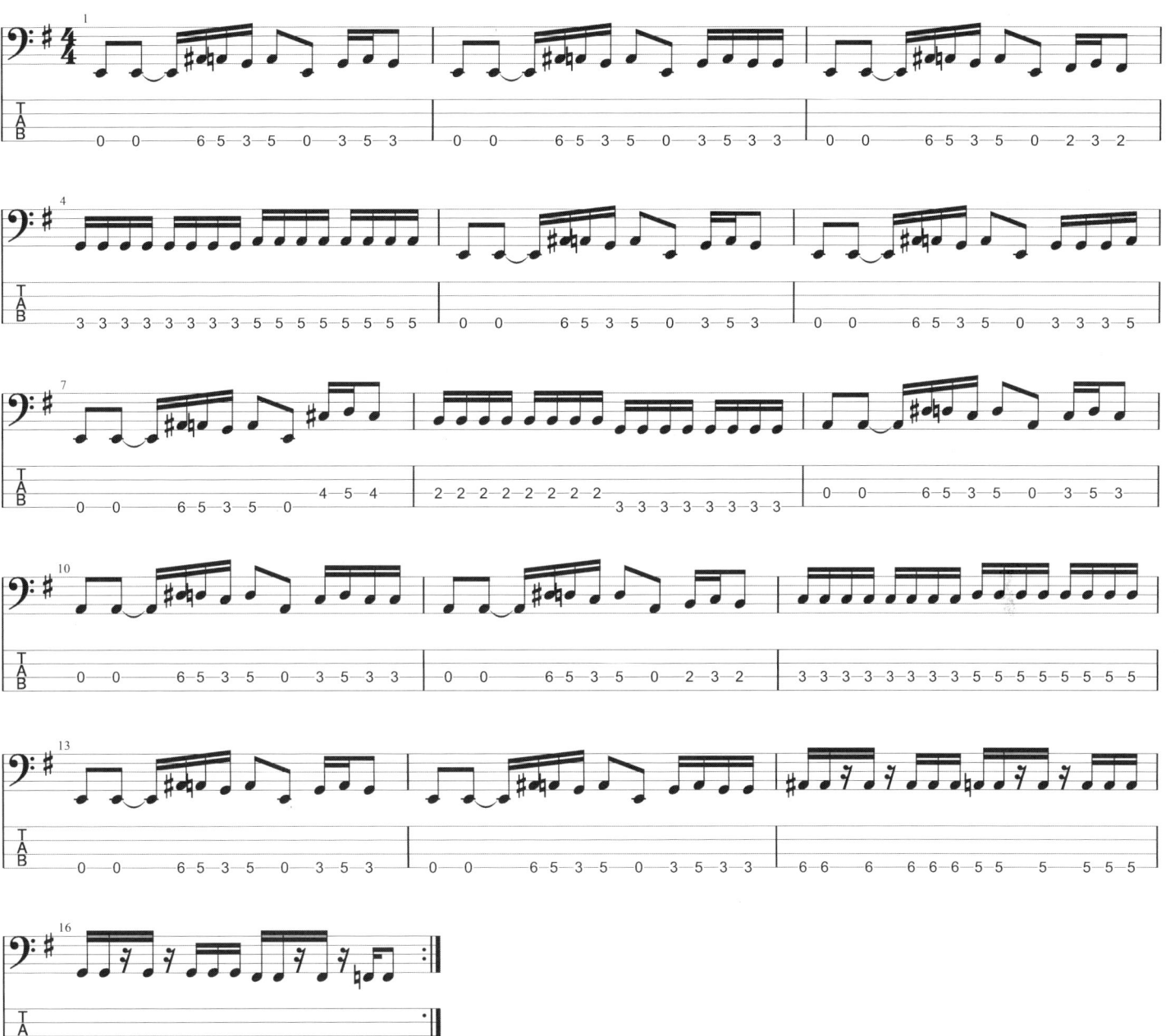

BASS GYM

42) 12-Bar Blues - Motown style

43) Soul Bassline in the style of James Jamerson

BASS GYM

44) Riff in the style of Rage Against the Machine

45) Hard Rock Dorian Bassline

101 POSITION EXERCISES (BEGINNER & INTERMEDIATE LEVEL)

BASS GYM

46) Disco Groove in the style of Jamiroquai

47) Blues Rock Riff using 'Blue' Notes

BASS GYM

48) Country Accompaniment

49) Breakbeat Accompaniment

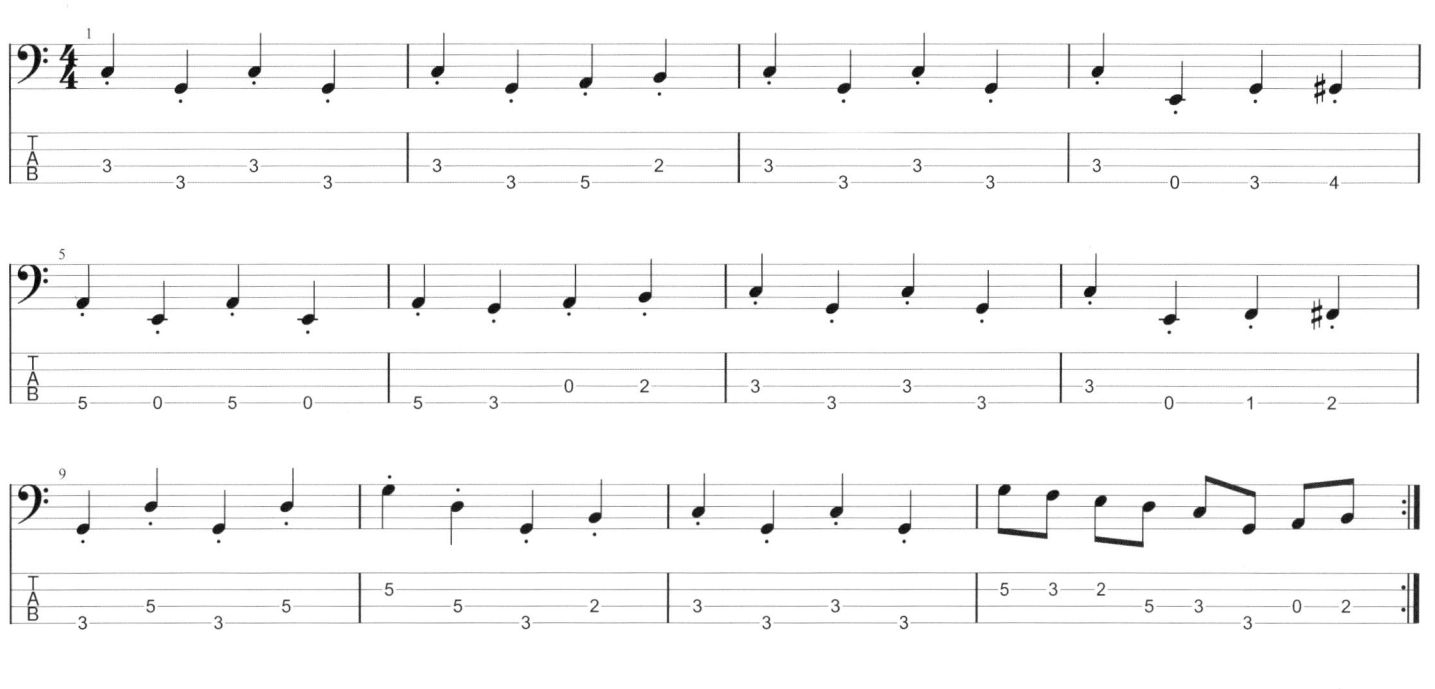

101 POSITION EXERCISES (BEGINNER & INTERMEDIATE LEVEL)

BASS GYM

50) Trip Hop Bassline Variations

42 101 POSITION EXERCISES (BEGINNER & INTERMEDIATE LEVEL)

BASS GYM

51) Walking Bassline (Combination of 2nd and 3rd Positions)

101 POSITION EXERCISES (BEGINNER & INTERMEDIATE LEVEL)

BASS GYM

52) Afrobeat

53) 12-Bar Minor Blues (in the style of 'The Thrill Is Gone')

BASS GYM

54) Pop Bassline

55) Rock Bassline in the style of 'Livin' On A Prayer' (Bon Jovi)

101 POSITION EXERCISES (BEGINNER & INTERMEDIATE LEVEL)

BASS GYM

56) Reggae Bassline in the style of 'Englishman In New York' (Sting)

46 101 POSITION EXERCISES (BEGINNER & INTERMEDIATE LEVEL)

BASS GYM

57) Octave Study

101 POSITION EXERCISES (BEGINNER & INTERMEDIATE LEVEL)

BASS GYM

58) 80s-style Pop Bassline

BASS GYM

59) Pop Rock Ballad

BASS GYM

60) Walking Bassline - 12-Bar Jazz Blues

BASS GYM

61) Funky Groove in the style of 'Get Lucky' - Daft Punk (combination of 3rd and 4th position)

101 POSITION EXERCISES (BEGINNER & INTERMEDIATE LEVEL)

BASS GYM

62) Folk Bassline

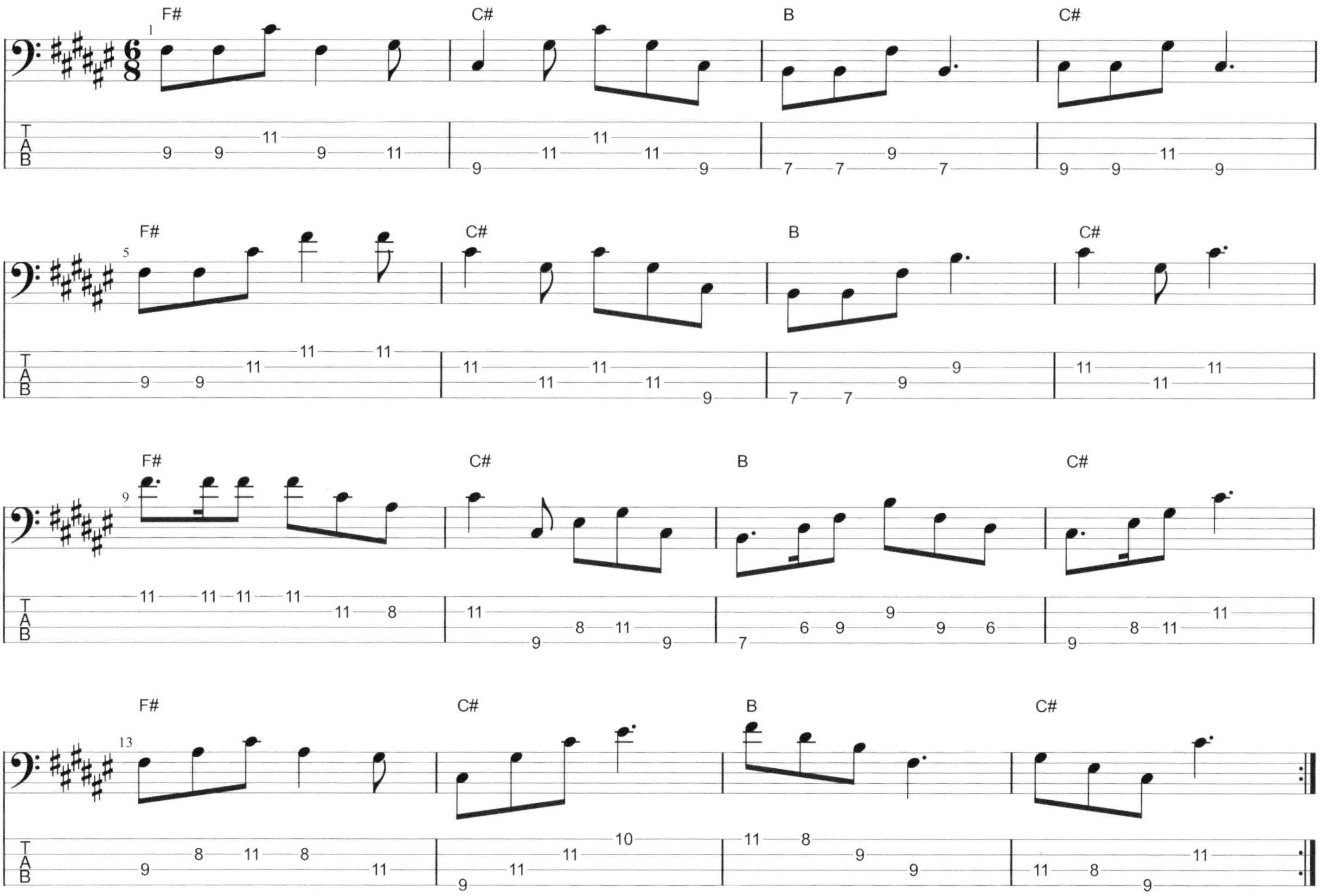

63) Neo Soul Groove

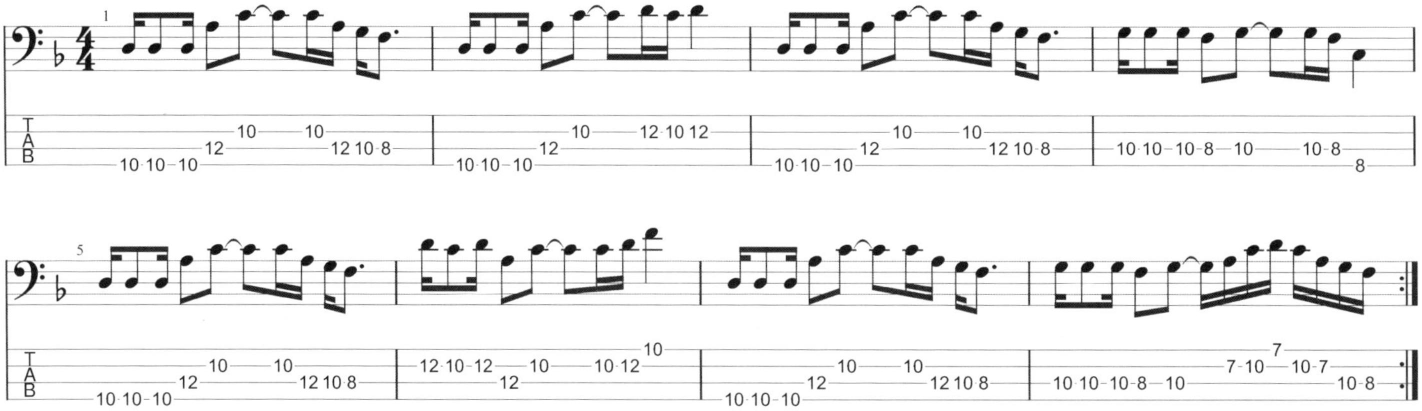

BASS GYM

64) Ska Bassline in the style of Madness

101 POSITION EXERCISES (BEGINNER & INTERMEDIATE LEVEL)

BASS GYM

65) New Wave Melodic Bassline with Double Stops

54   101 POSITION EXERCISES (BEGINNER & INTERMEDIATE LEVEL)

BASS GYM

66) Aeolian Techno Bassline

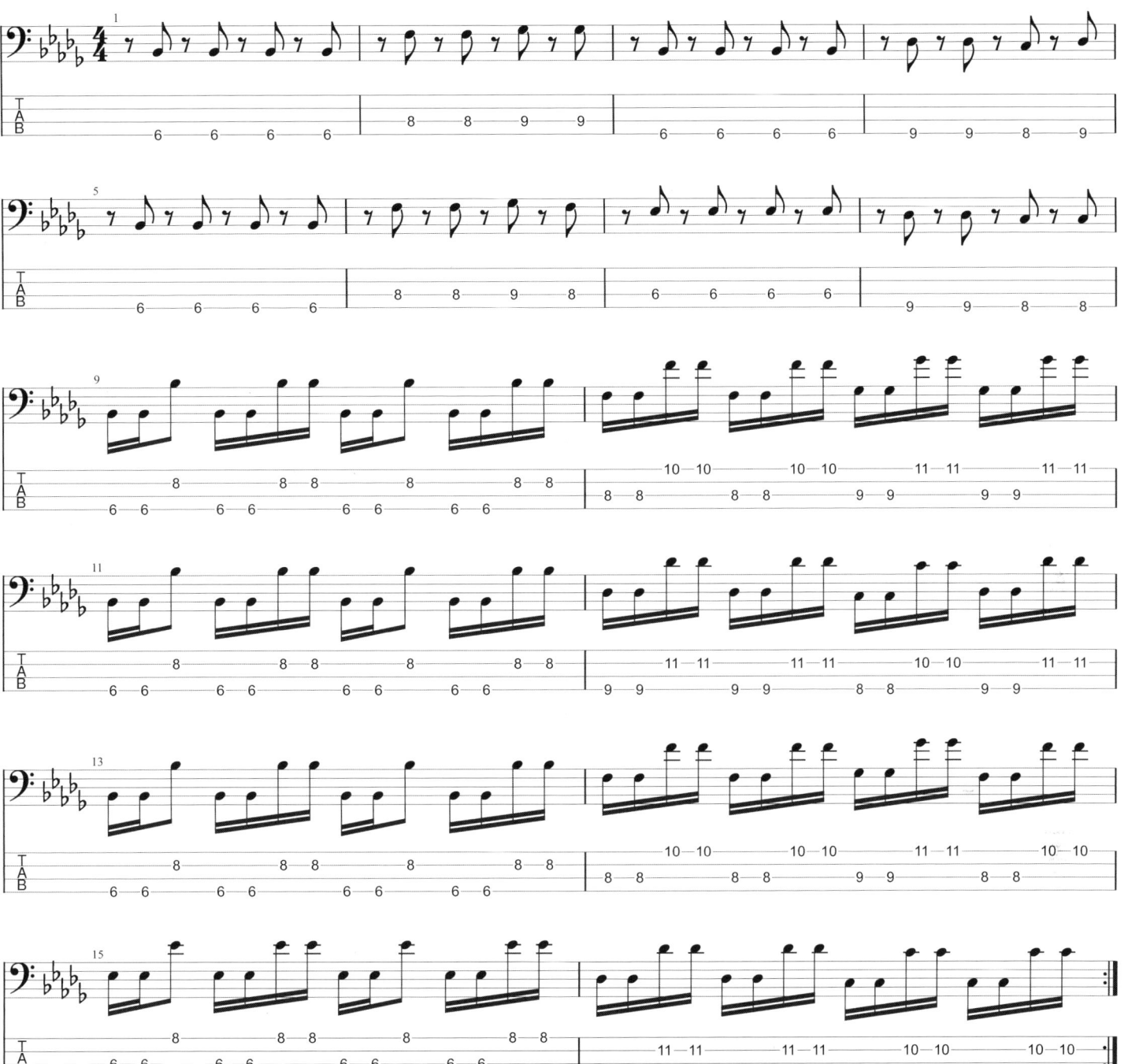

101 POSITION EXERCISES (BEGINNER & INTERMEDIATE LEVEL)

BASS GYM

67) Underground House Bassline

BASS GYM

68) Guajira - Salsa Bassline

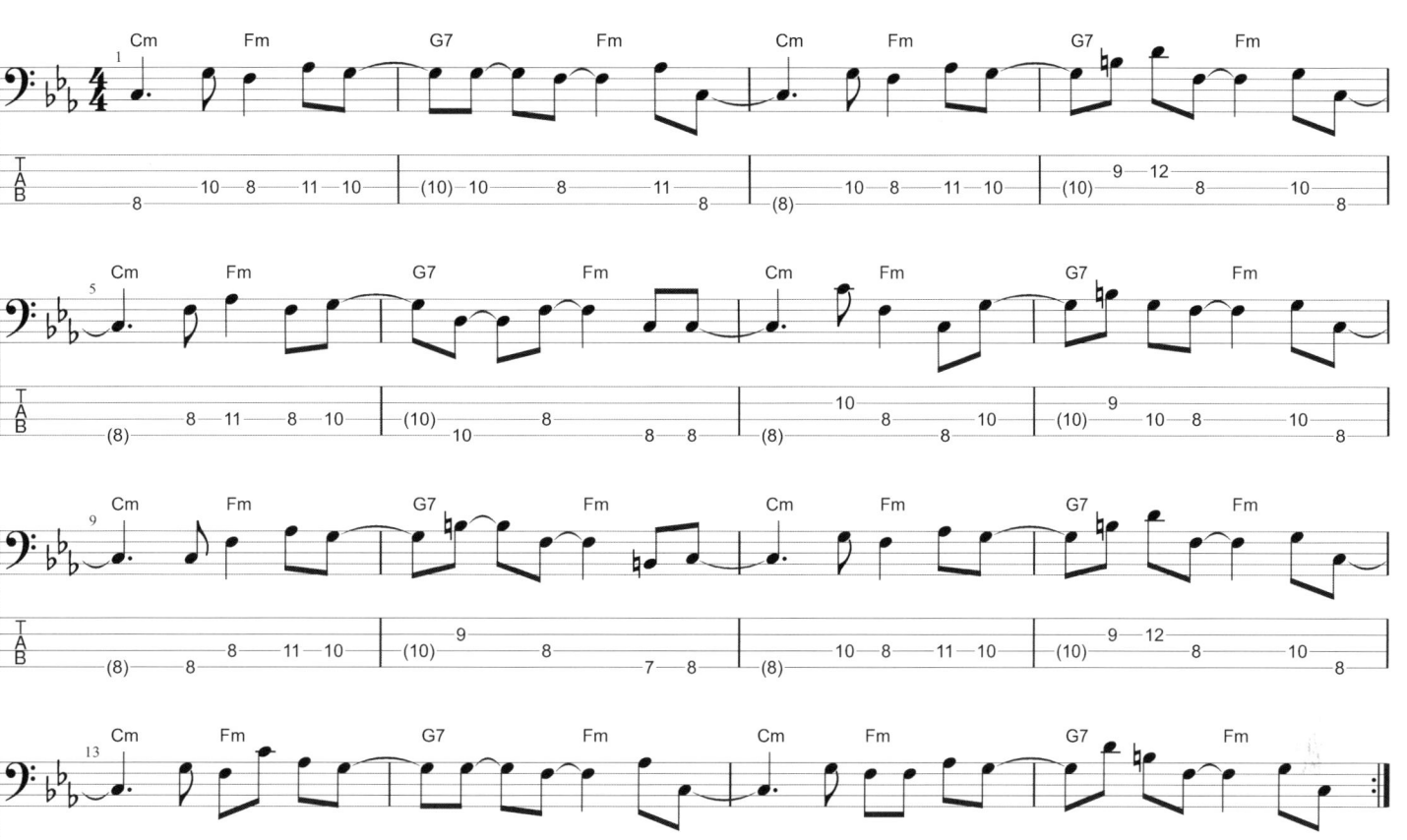

BASS GYM

69) Guaracha - Salsa Bassline

58   101 POSITION EXERCISES (BEGINNER & INTERMEDIATE LEVEL)

BASS GYM

70) Reggae Bassline in Rock Steady Style

71) Rhythm 'n' Blues (Skipping between 1st and 3rd Position)

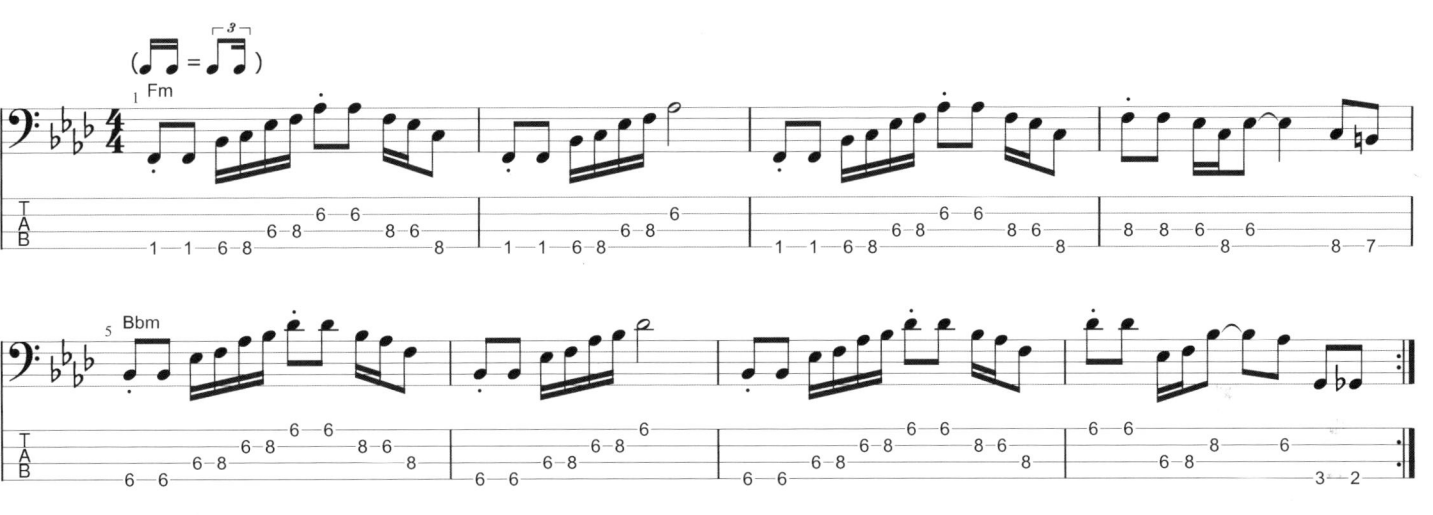

72) Stoner Rock Riff with Tritones

BASS GYM

73) Rock riff in the style of Foo Fighters

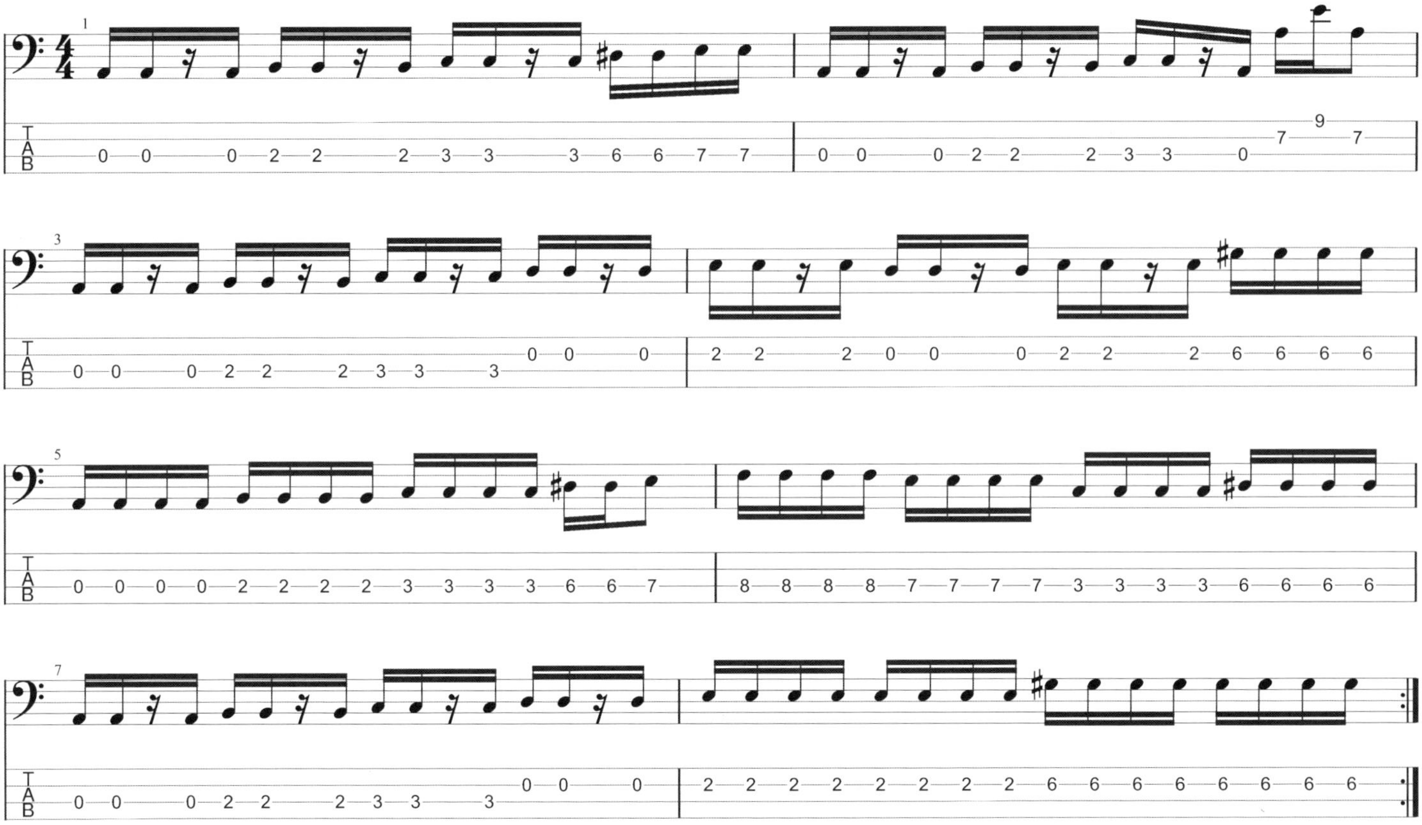

74) Neo Soul Groove

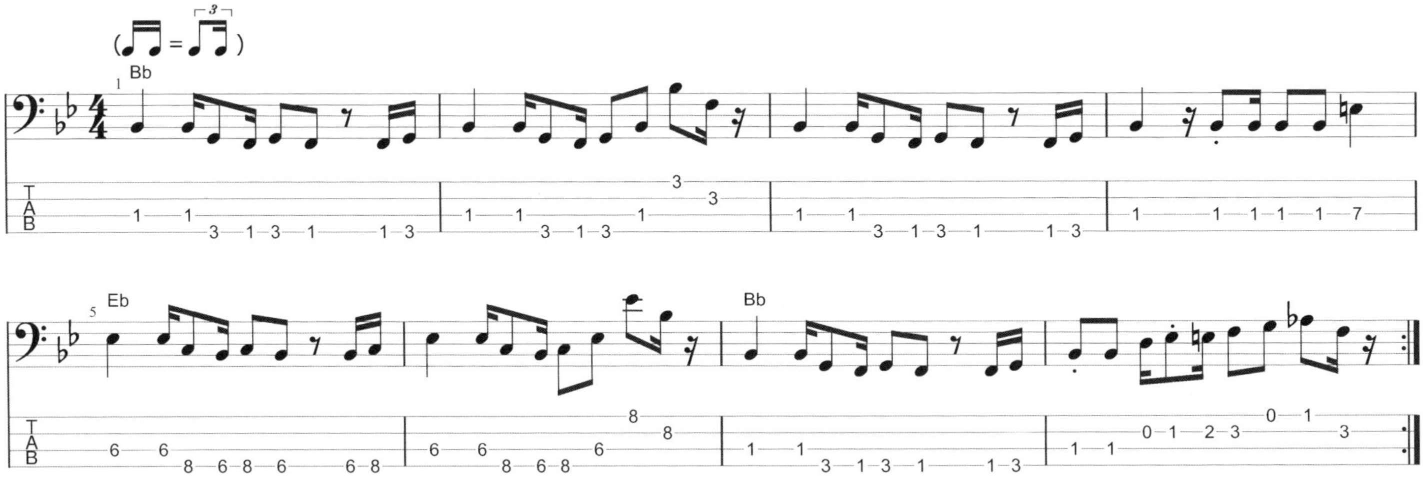

BASS GYM

75) Funk Rock in RATM style

76) New Orleans Funk - G Mixolydian (skipping between 2nd and 4th position)

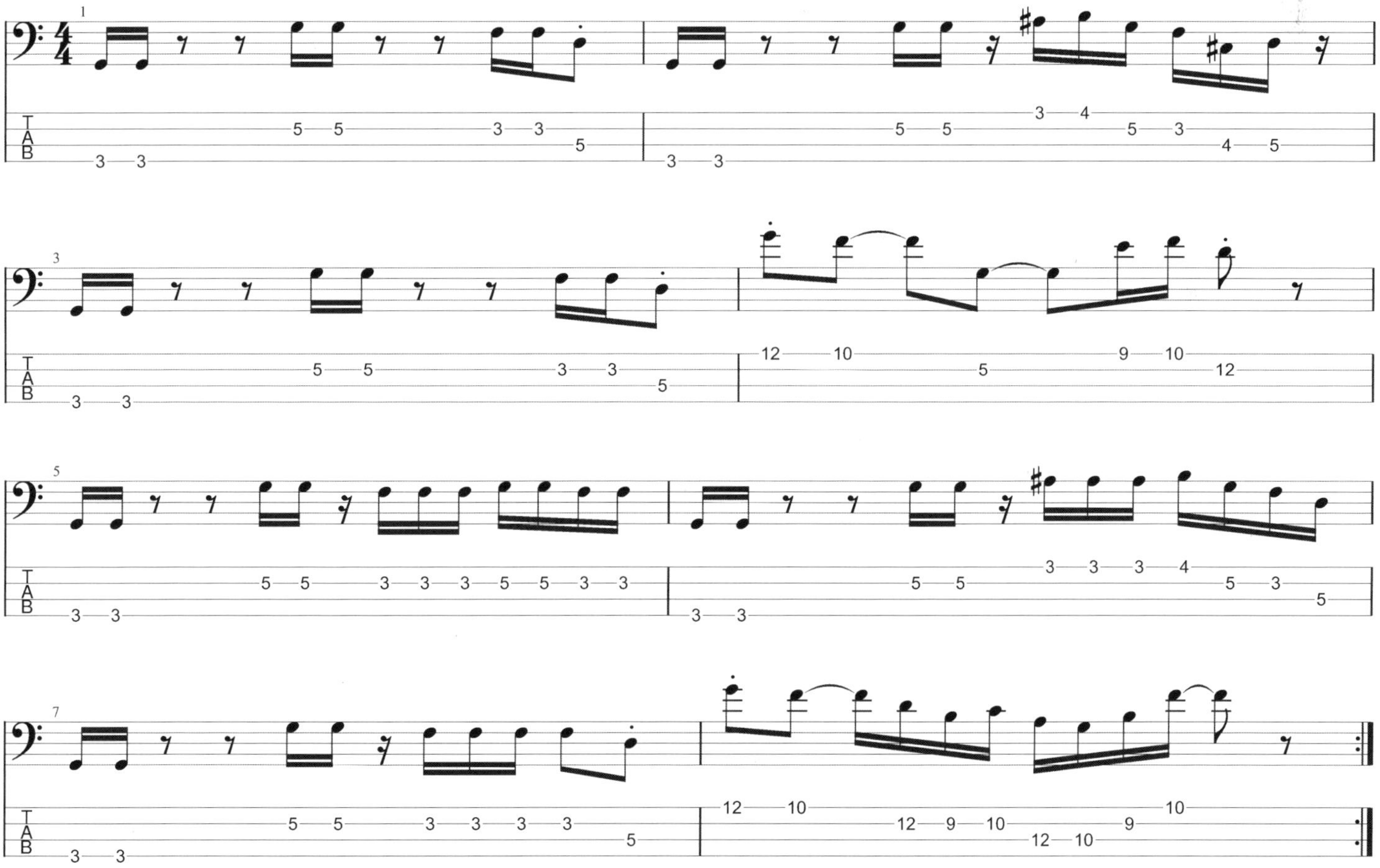

101 POSITION EXERCISES (BEGINNER & INTERMEDIATE LEVEL)

BASS GYM

77) Harmonic Minor Progressive Bassline

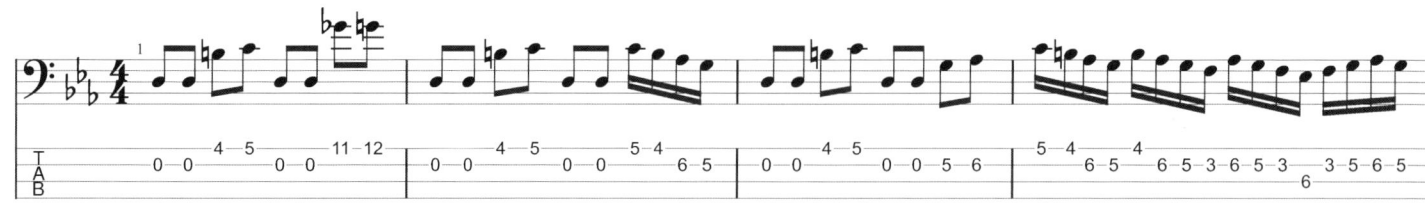
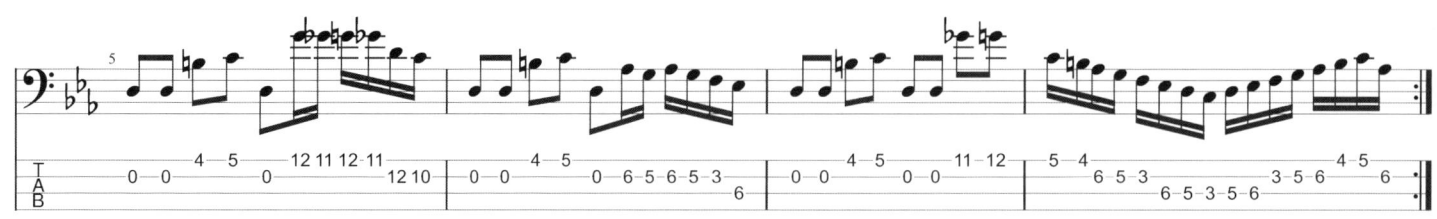

78) Fusion Groove

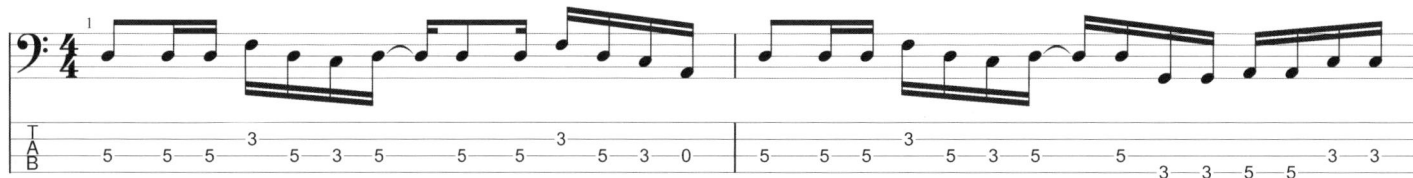
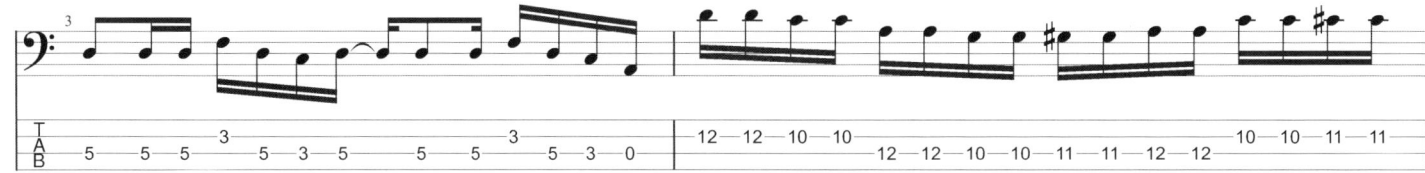
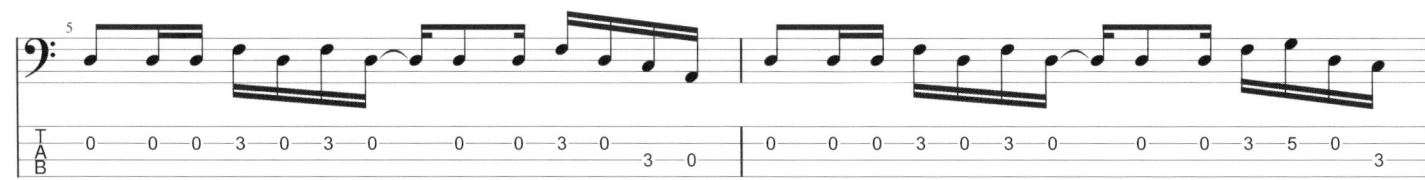
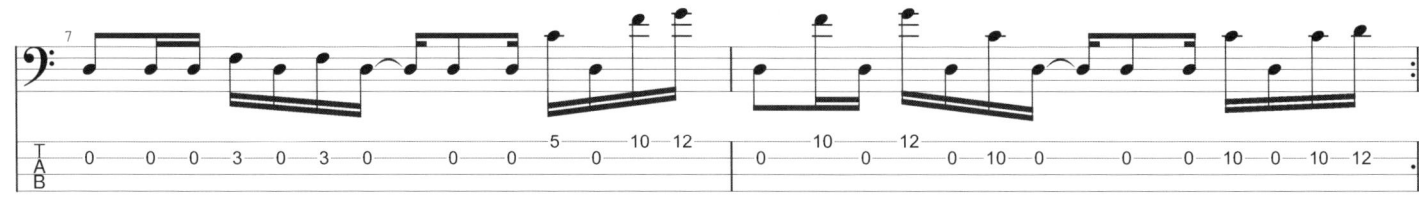

79) Funky Groove in the style of Maceo Parker

BASS GYM

80) Blues Rock Riff

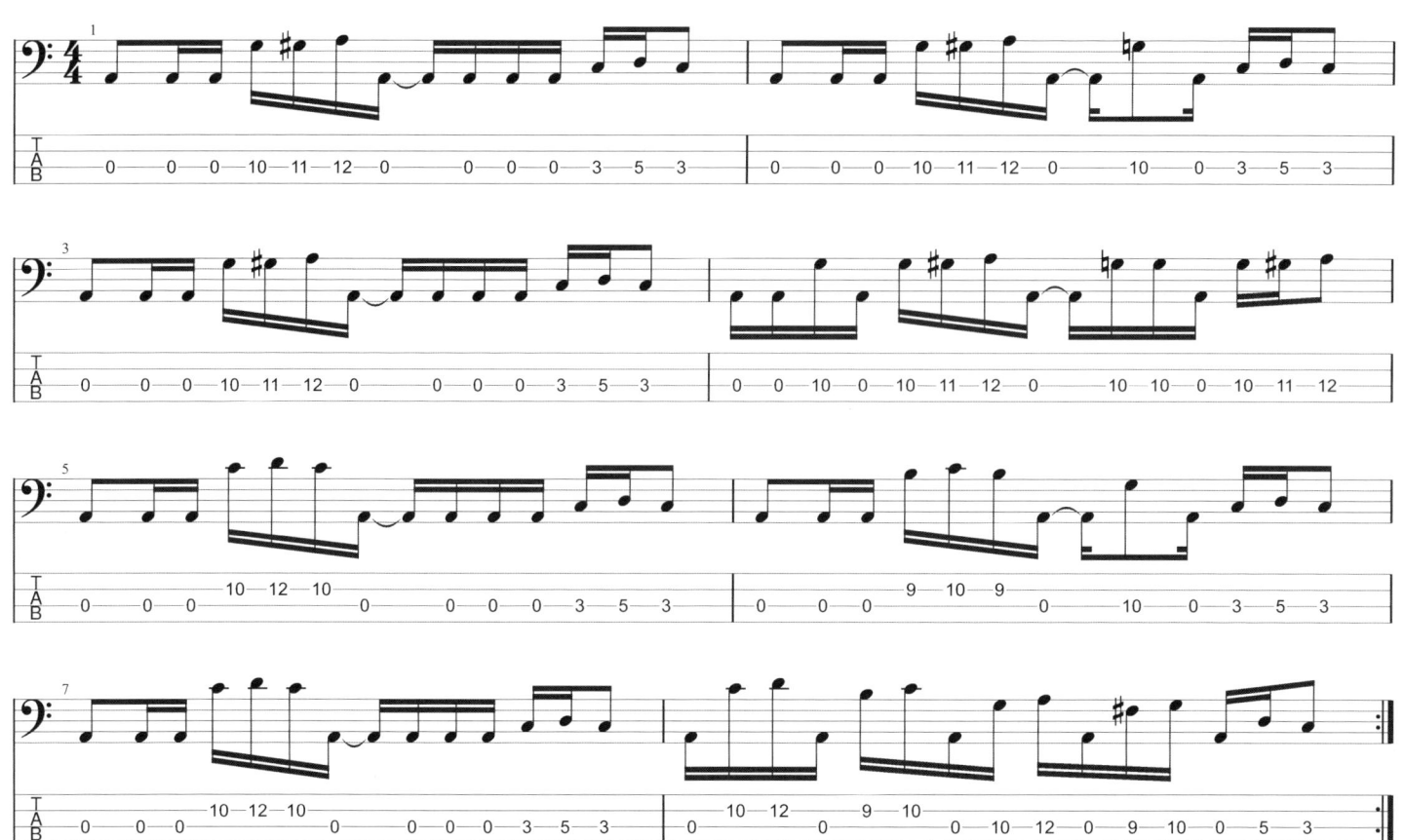

BASS GYM

81) Arpeggio Variations (Skipping between 1st and 4th Position)

82) Pop Rock Riff

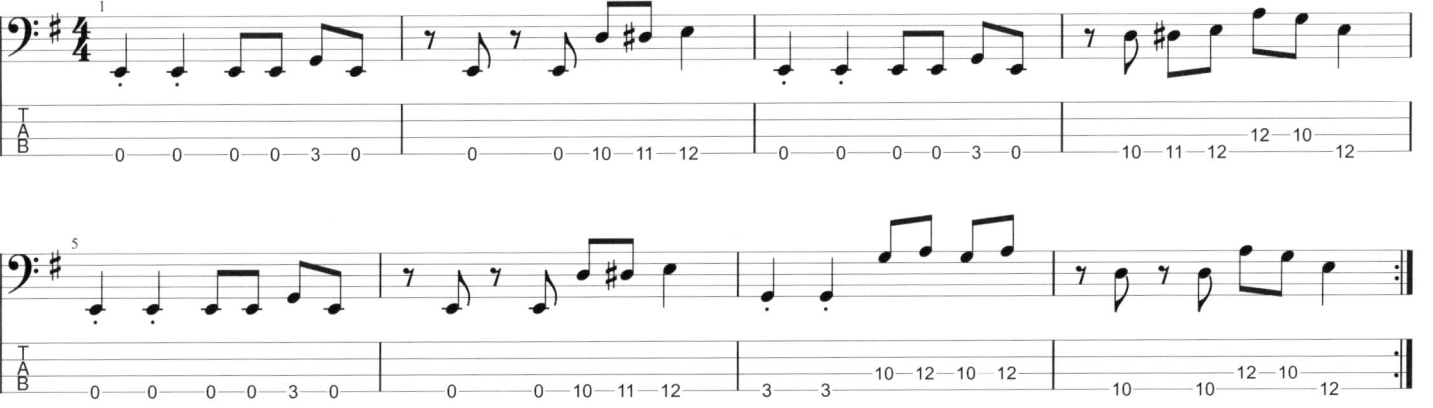

101 POSITION EXERCISES (BEGINNER & INTERMEDIATE LEVEL)

BASS GYM

83) Melodic Punk Bassline

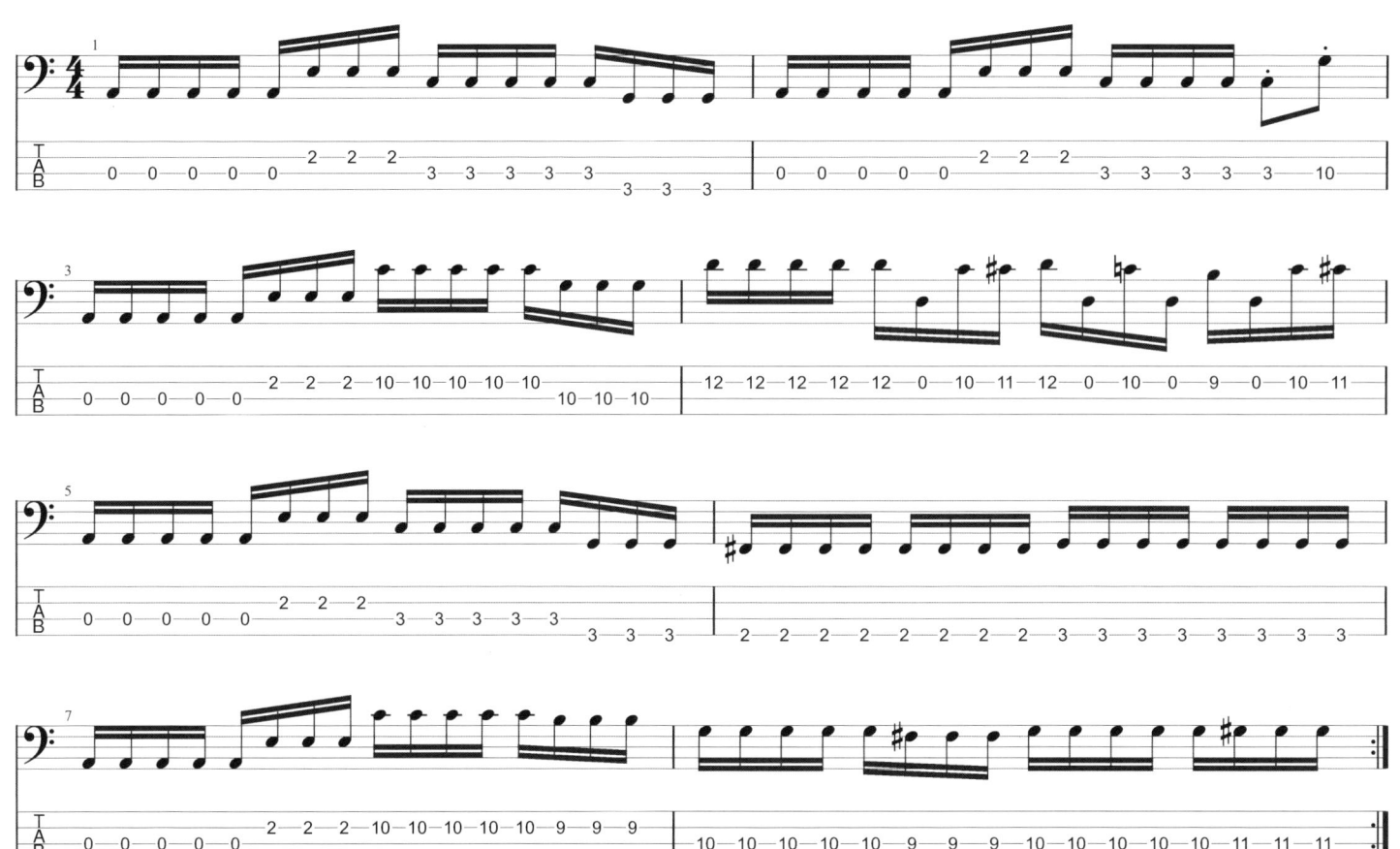

BASS GYM

84) Progressive Dream Theater Style Riff

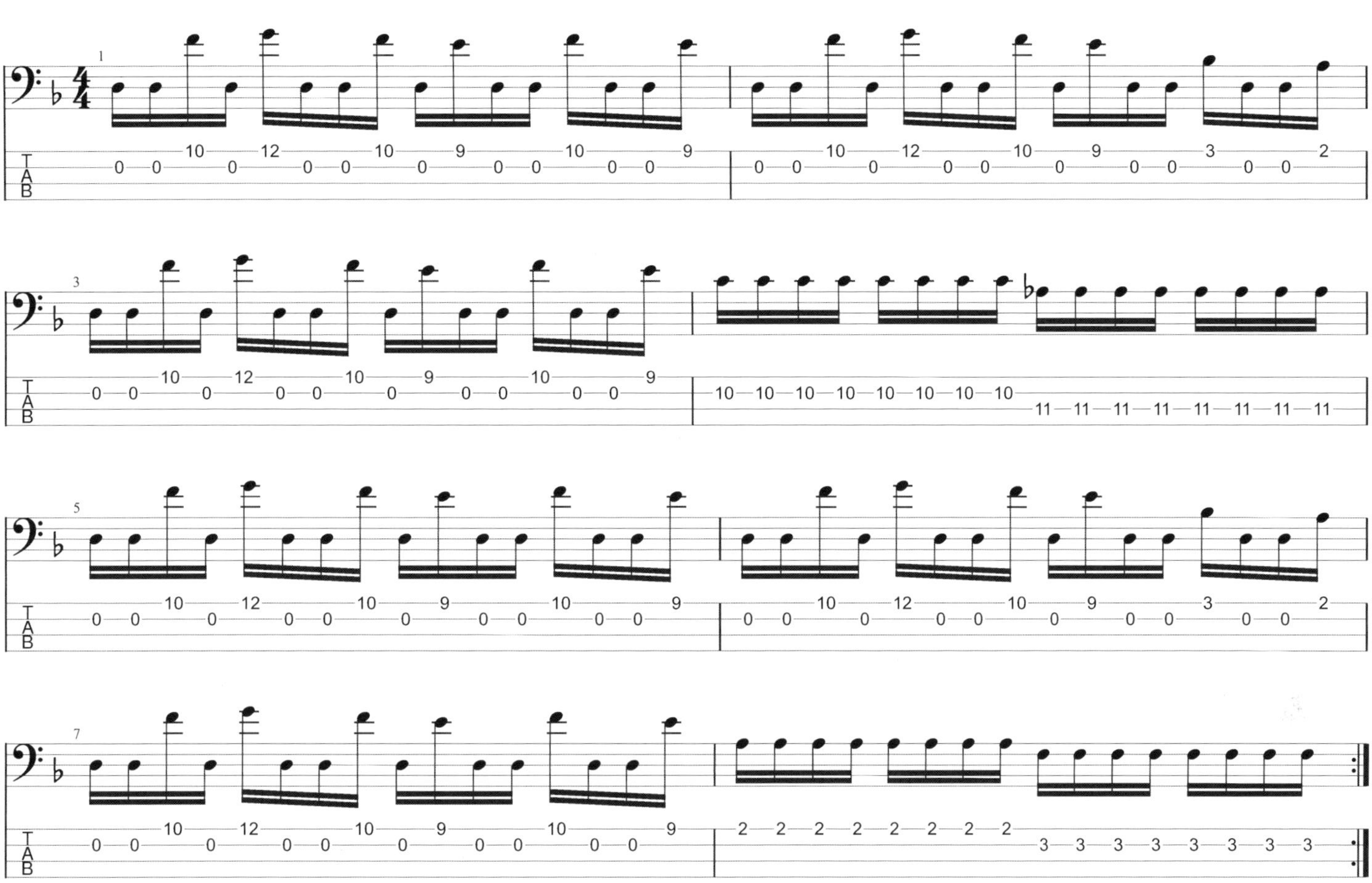

85) Reggae Bassline

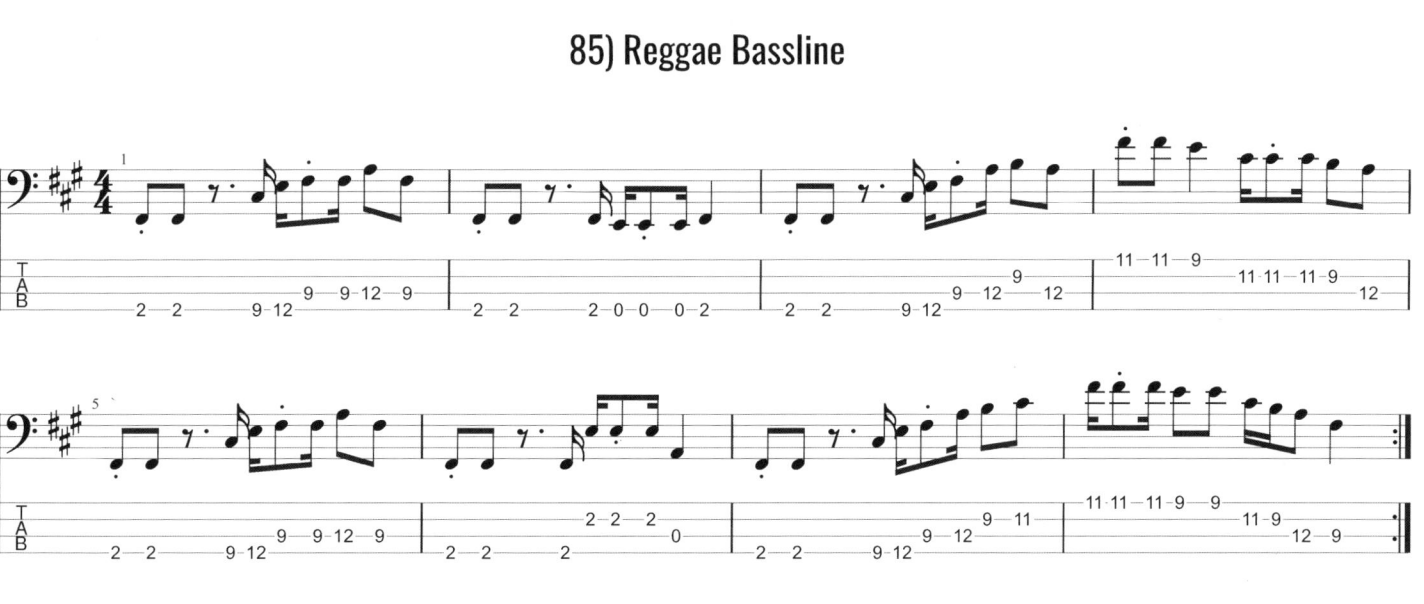

101 POSITION EXERCISES (BEGINNER & INTERMEDIATE LEVEL)

BASS GYM

86) G7 Walking Bassline Variations (Linking 1st, 2nd, 3rd and 4th Positions)

BASS GYM

87) EDM Bassline

BASS GYM

88) Bass Riff in the style of 'Hysteria' (Muse)

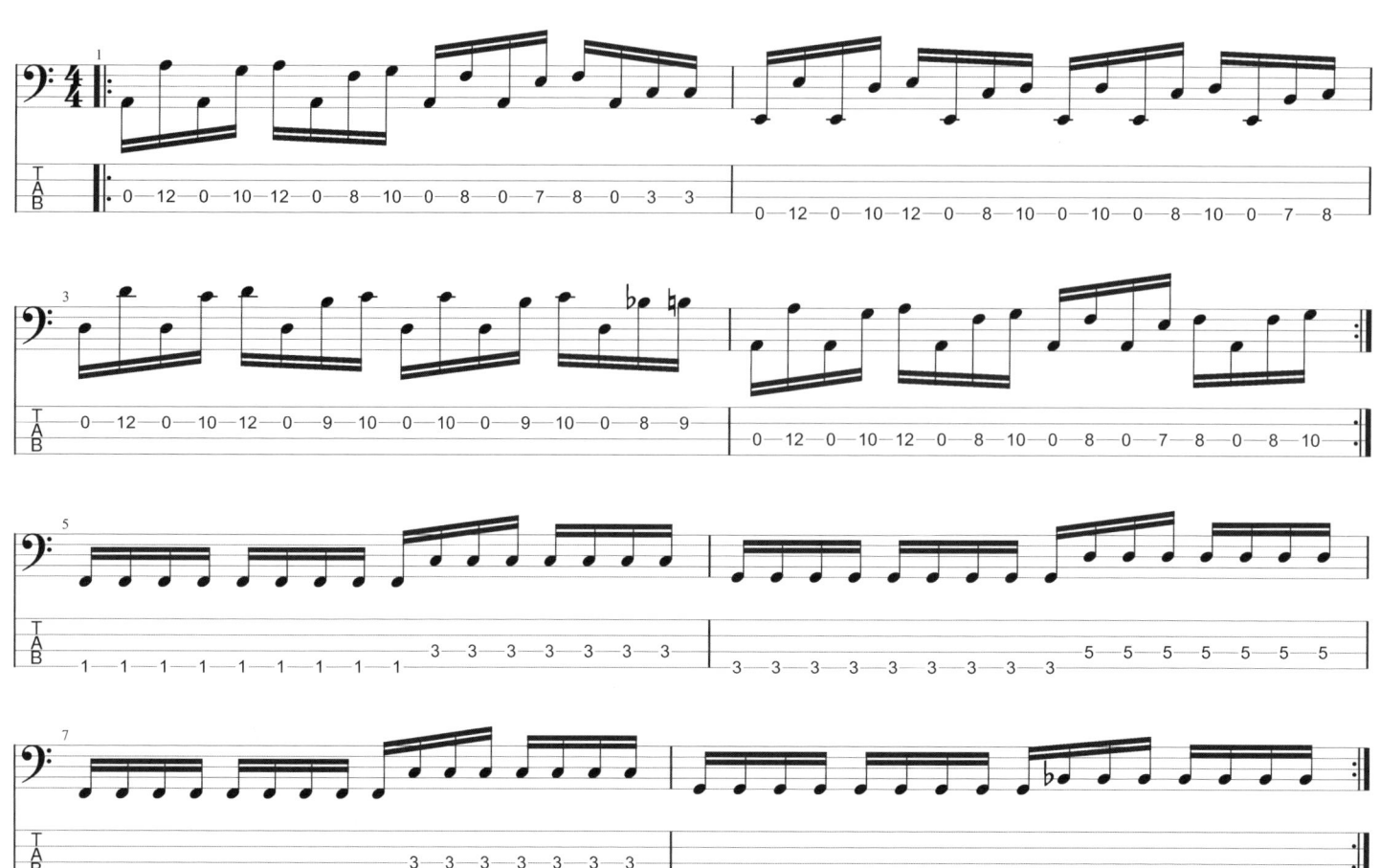

BASS GYM

89) Neoclassical Etude

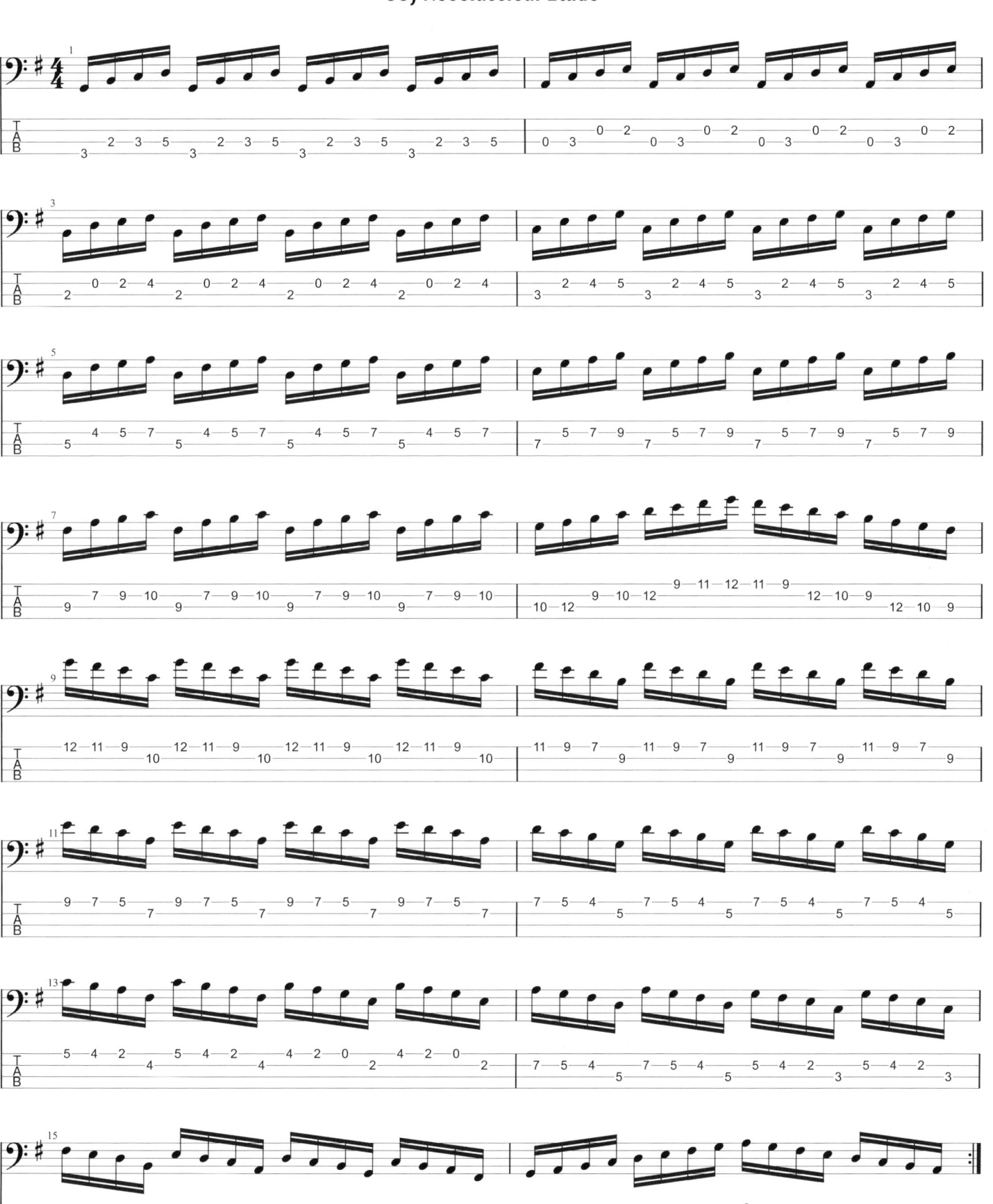

101 POSITION EXERCISES (BEGINNER & INTERMEDIATE LEVEL)

BASS GYM

90) Vulfpeck-style 12-Bar Soul Blues

BASS GYM

91) Bluegrass Cherokee Shuffle Bassline

101 POSITION EXERCISES (BEGINNER & INTERMEDIATE LEVEL)

BASS GYM

92) Hip Hop Bassline

74 101 POSITION EXERCISES (BEGINNER & INTERMEDIATE LEVEL)

BASS GYM

93) Rhythm and Blues Bassline

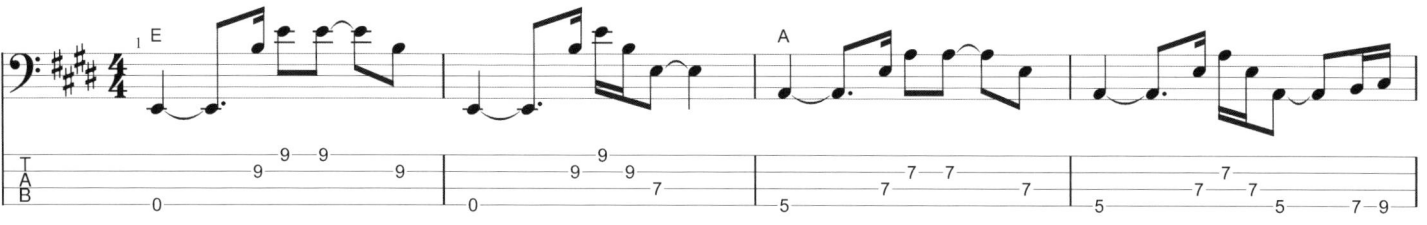
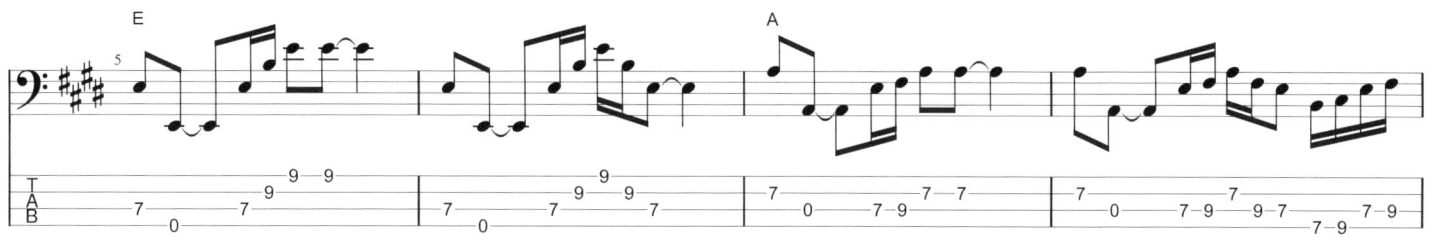
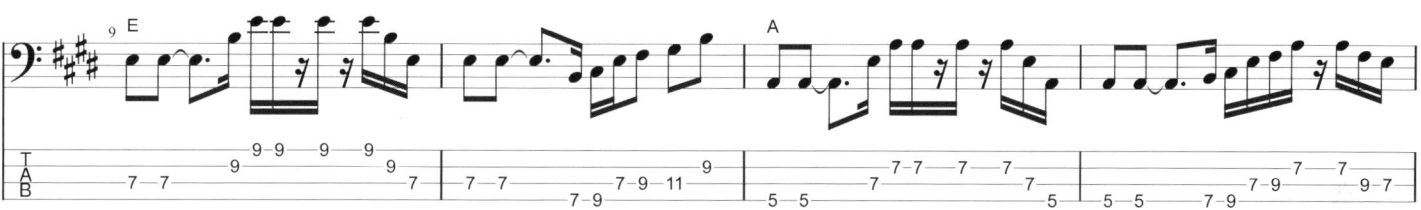
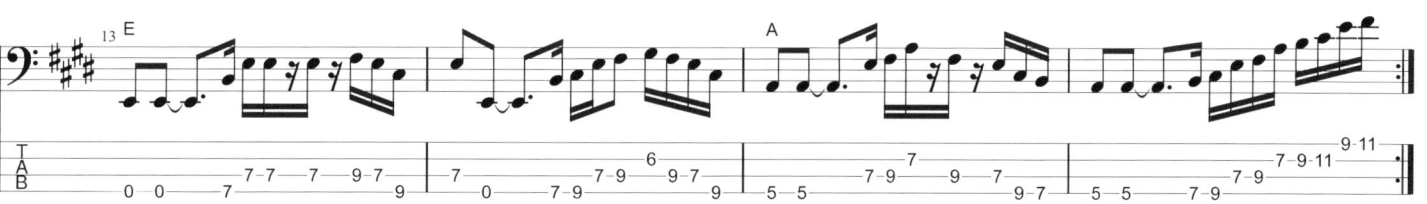

101 POSITION EXERCISES (BEGINNER & INTERMEDIATE LEVEL)

BASS GYM

94) Bossa Nova Variations

76 101 POSITION EXERCISES (BEGINNER & INTERMEDIATE LEVEL)

BASS GYM

95) Pop Bassline on Most Common Progression

101 POSITION EXERCISES (BEGINNER & INTERMEDIATE LEVEL) 77

BASS GYM

96) Eighth Note Bassline with Melodic Variations

BASS GYM

97) Pop Rock Bassline

98) Staccato R&B Bassline

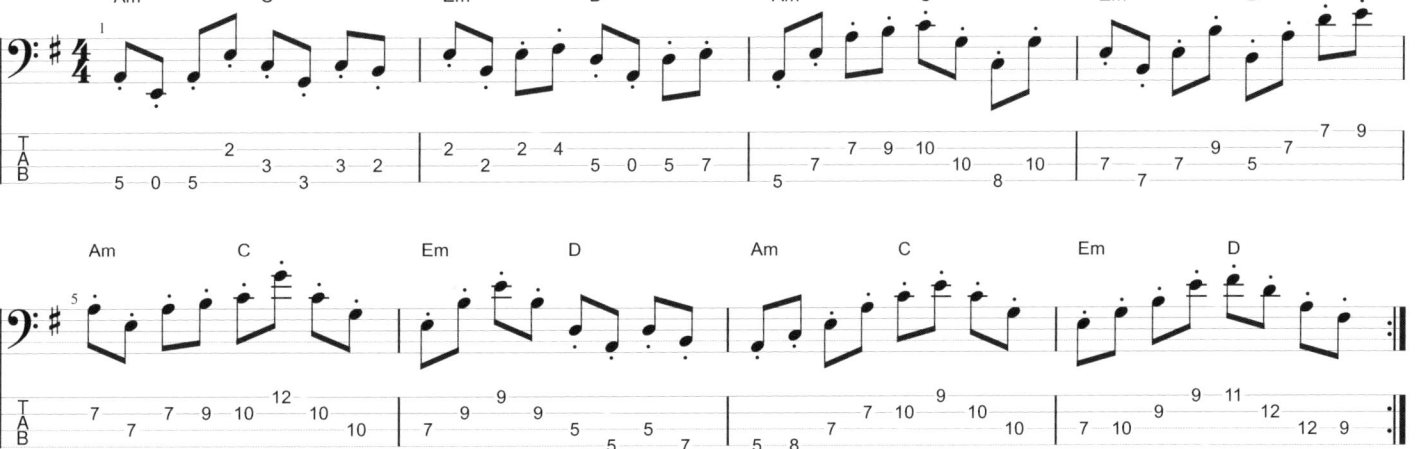

BASS GYM

99) Melodic String Skipping Variations

80   101 POSITION EXERCISES (BEGINNER & INTERMEDIATE LEVEL)

BASS GYM

100) Arpeggios in Salsa Style

BASS GYM

101) Funky Fusion Groove

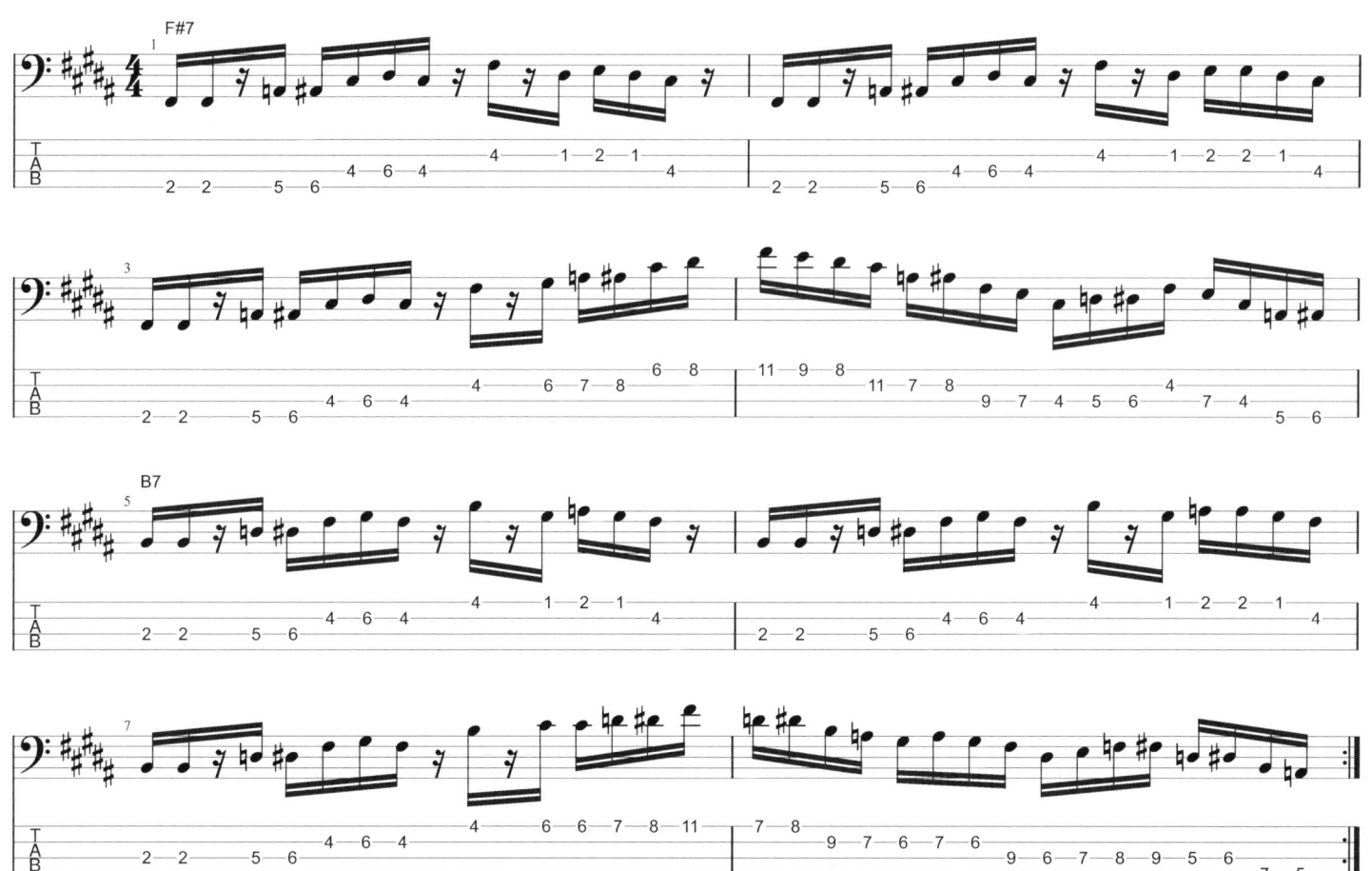

82 101 POSITION EXERCISES (BEGINNER & INTERMEDIATE LEVEL)

Bassline Publishing Theory & Technique Books

The following theory and technique books are available from Bassline Publishing

The Bass Guitarist's Guide to Reading Music - Beginner Level

The Bass Guitarist's Guide to Reading Music - Intermediate Level

The Bass Guitarist's Guide to Reading Music - Advanced Level

The Bass Guitarist's Guide to Scales & Modes

Play Bass

Ultimate Slap Bass

100 Slap Bass Grooves

Ultimate Tapping for Bass Guitar

Plectrum Technique for Bass Guitar

Bass Lick of the Week

Beginner Studies for Bass Guitar

Intermediate Studies for Bass Guitar

Advanced Studies for Bass Guitar

Giants of Bass Vol. 1 - 60s & 70s

Giants of Bass Vol. 2 - 80s & 90s

The Bassist's Guide to Injury Management, Prevention & Better Health - Vol. 1

The Bassist's Guide to Injury Management, Prevention & Better Health - Vol. 2

The Bassist's Complete Guide to Injury Management, Prevention & Better Health

Available to order from
www.basslinepublishing.com
and from

ALSO AVAILABLE BASSLINE PUBLISHING VIDEO COURSES

After many years of writing a popular series of bass guitar tuition and transcription books, author and leading bass educator Stuart Clayton has created a series of instructional video courses. These are available via subscription to users all over the world.

Informed by Stuart's extensive experience as a teacher at one of the UK's top music schools, these courses are broken down into short, manageable lessons, with clear, attainable goals. Users can subscribe monthly or annually - subscriptions can be cancelled at any time.

MONTHLY* Subscription £7.99 per month
ANNUAL* Subscription £89 per year

Video Courses include:

Giants of Bass
Each course contains a full play-through of the piece, followed by section-by-section lessons on how to play in the style of well-known bassists including Billy Sheehan, Bootsy Collins, Carol Kaye, Flea, Mark King and many more.

Learning the Modes
This series of courses takes each of the modes and breaks it down into detail. Each course covers approaches to playing the mode all over the fingerboard and a range of exercises that it to use, so that you can hear the unique sound that each one offers.

Slap Bass
Beginner, Intermediate & Advanced
These courses are based on the popular Ultimate Slap Bass book and cover everything you need about this technique!

Scales and Arpeggios
Learn using the 'content over patterns' theory, avoiding the use of patterns and box shapes, and instead focuses on the notes.

Plectrum Course
This is a crucial technique to master for any professional bassist and this course is the perfect place to start.

Song Tutorials
Popular songs are broken down, section by section. Includes: 'Tommy the Cat' (Primus), 'Forget Me Nots' (Patrice Rushen), 'The Machine Stops' (Level 42), 'Hump de Bump' (Red Hot Chili Peppers) and more.

Tapping
Tapping is a rather unconventional technique, but in the right hands, it can be a valuable musical tool. Learn finger dexterity exercises, muting, and the best way to set up your bass for this technique.

New courses added regularly!

www.basslinepublishing.com

*Prices correct at time of printing but may be subject to change.

Made in United States
Orlando, FL
12 December 2024

55260208R00048